101
DEFENSIVE
BASEBALL
DRILLS

Pat McMahon
James A. Peterson

ISBN: 1-58518-346-6

Library of Congress Catalog Card Number: 2001095648

Cover and text design: Rebecca Gold

Front cover photo: Courtesy of The University of Florida
                         Sports Information Office
Back cover photo: Courtesy of USA Baseball

Coaches Choice
P.O. Box 1828
Monterey, CA 93942
www.coacheschoice.com

To my family, especially my dad, Jack, and my mom, Pat, you are my "first coaches."

To my wife, Cheri, and Logan, my daughter, and J. Wells, my son. I love you. You make me a better person each day.

ACKNOWLEDGMENTS

To all the coaches, players, managers, and trainers I have had the privilege of playing under and working with, you have taught me so much. *Thank you!*

CONTENTS

Chapters

PREFACE

I wrote this book to provide baseball coaches at all competitive levels with a tool that can enable them to maximize the skills and potential of their players. As a vehicle for teaching and learning, properly designed and applied drills can have extraordinary value. Coaches should keep in mind, however, that to a great extent, drills are like medicine. The proper prescription can help a player in countless ways. In that regard, each coach has the ultimate responsibility to administer the "medicine" at the right time, in the right amount, and in the right way.

As such, every drill should be conducted in a "learning atmosphere," where each player is given an opportunity to be successful. When an athlete performs well, he should be praised. On the other hand, when his performance does not measure up to expectations, he should be given constructive feedback that enables him to refocus his energies and efforts in such a manner to achieve the desired goal.

Each of the two volumes of drills in this series *101 Offensive Baseball Drills* and *101 Defensive Baseball Drills* features drills that I have collected and field-tested over the course of my coaching career. If in the process of using the drills presented in this book coaches are better able to develop the abilities and essential attributes of their players, then the effort to write these two drill books will have been well worthwhile.

— Pat McMahon

Direction of Player	⟶
Thrown Ball	----⟶
Batted Ball	∿∿∿⟶
Rolled Ball	⋯⋯⋯⟶
Coach	x
Players	○
Target	▦
Catcher	●
Wall or Fence	___
Base	☐
Cones	△

CHAPTER 1

INFIELDER DRILLS

DRILL # 1: READY, SET, GO!

Objective: To develop player reaction time and footwork; to reinforce the mechanics of the proper ready position.

Equipment Needed: None required (although players can use gloves).

Description: Players line up in rows approximately arms-length apart from each other facing the coach. Upon command from the coach, the players assume a ready position—weight on the balls of their feet, prepared to move immediately in any direction. The coach makes necessary corrections and/or adjustments in the ready positions of the players. The coach then blows a short burst on his whistle and points in the direction he wants the players to move. The players instantly sprint five yards in that direction and resume the ready position facing the coach. The coach can either have the players relax before resuming the drill or point in a new direction to continue the drill immediately.

Coaching Points:

- The coach can vary the drill by either requiring the players to crossover or push off when initiating lateral movements or adjusting the length or nature of the required movement.

- This drill may be used as a warm-up exercise.

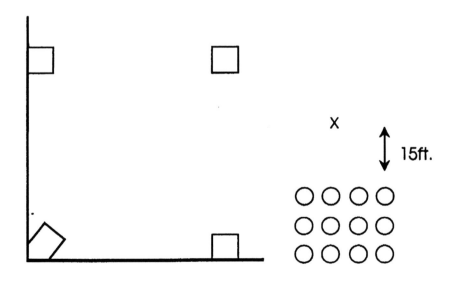

DRILL # 2: STEP-REACTION DRILL

Objective: To develop footwork, enhance kinesthetic awareness, improve fielding mechanics, and practice throwing skills.

Equipment Needed: Gloves and one baseball per two players.

Description: Working in pairs, the players start on the foul line about 25 feet apart facing each other. The player closest to home plate starts the drill by rolling the ball 10 to 15 feet to the center field side of his partner. Using a crossover step, his partner moves to the ball, fields it, cushions it to his belt and throws it back to the player who started the drill. Both players continue the drill in this fashion until they have moved approximately 150 feet in a straight line toward center field. The players then return to the end of the line, and the drill continues.

Coaching Points:

- Players can vary the type and speed of the rolled (thrown) ball to be fielded.

- Competition can be created by either timing two pairs' repetitions and naming the fastest team the winner or by awarding points for each successfully fielded ball.

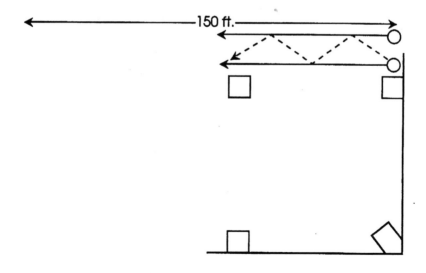

DRILL # 3: BALL ROTATION SPIN DRILL/FLUID ARM-ACTION

Objective: To develop and practice the proper mechanics and techniques of throwing.

Equipment Needed: Gloves and one "50/50" colored baseball per two players.

Description: Working in pairs, the players kneel down on one knee and face each other 40 to 60 feet apart. Using a specially colored baseball (half one color, half another), each player throws a ball to his partner, aiming at the receiving player's chest. Prior to throwing the ball, all players hold the ball by placing their first two fingers side-by-side on either side of the two colors of the ball (the midline) and their thumb exactly on the midline underneath the ball. As they throw the ball, the players should analyze the spin on the ball. If the midline of the two colors of the ball doesn't remain perpendicular to the ground while the ball is in flight, and if the colors don't stay side-by-side during the throw, the player making the throw should review where his fingers were placed on the ball and the position of his wrist while making the throw. While throwing, the wrist, elbow, and shoulder of the throwing arm should be relatively loose and flexible. It should never be tight and rigid. As the throwing arm is moved rearward to initiate the throwing motion, that arm should be fully extended in a non-rigid manner. Then, as the throwing arm is brought around, the flat (palm-side) portion of the wrist is completed by having the wrist flick the ball and the throwing shoulder follow-through.

Coaching Points:

- The coach should require each player to perform a specific number of properly executed throws.

- The coach can vary the drill by adjusting the distance the players kneel from each other.

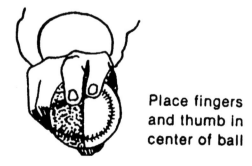

Place fingers and thumb in center of ball

DRILL # 4: THROWING FOR ACCURACY

Objective: To improve throwing mechanics and techniques; to develop throwing accuracy.

Equipment Needed: Gloves and one "50/50" colored baseball per two players.

Description: Working in pairs, the players stand 60 to 90 feet apart, facing one another. The drill begins by having a player throw to his partner, using a half-and-half colored baseball. The player attempts to throw the ball to the center of his partner's chest. His partner catches the throw with two hands and holds his glove exactly where he caught the ball so that the accuracy of the throw (relative to its position in the chest area) can be readily seen. Points are given to the thrower based upon where the ball is caught: chest = five points, head = three points, legs = one point, and one point is subtracted for any throw away from the receiver's body. A running total of points earned is kept. The first player to earn a predetermined number of points wins the drill competition.

Coaching Points:

- Players should analyze the spin on the balls that they throw. On properly held and thrown balls, the two colors will remain on opposite sides and the center division line will remain perpendicular to the ground while the ball is in flight.

- Coaches should analyze the throwing mechanics and techniques of the players and make corrections as appropriate.

- The drill can be varied by having a player throw the ball after fielding a thrown ground ball.

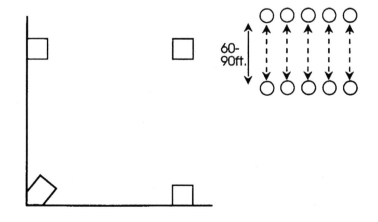

DRILL # 5: EASY RHYTHM

Objective: To enhance the "blending" of the mechanics of fielding into a smooth (coordinated) effort.

Equipment Needed: Gloves and one baseball for every two players.

Description: Working in pairs, the players stand 70 to 90 feet apart facing one another. The drill begins by having one player (A) roll (throw) various types of ground balls to his partner (B). Player B fields the ground ball and, using the skip-and-throw technique throws it back to A. Player B's throw is directed at the chest of A. Player A catches the throw and continues the drill by rolling another ground ball at B. The players switch roles after player B has fielded 10 balls.

Coaching Points:

- Coaches should make corrections in the fielding and throwing mechanics of the players as appropriate.

- Coaches should emphasize the need to assume a proper ready position before fielding a ground ball and should reinforce the techniques involved in properly moving to a ground ball to field it.

- Coaches can speed up the drill by having the players stand closer together (i.e., 20 feet apart) when facing each other.

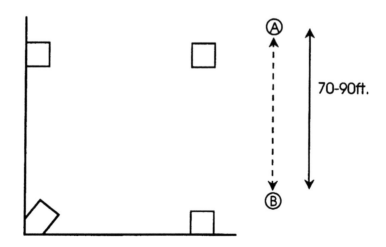

DRILL # 6: SHORT HOP

Objective: To improve glove action; to practice fielding short hops.

Equipment Needed: Gloves and one baseball for every two players.

Description: Working in pairs, the players stand apart facing one another. The distance they stand apart varies according to whether the drill is focusing on short hops (i.e., five to seven feet) or on a longer distance (i.e., 30 to 50 feet). The players throw difficult short hops to each other that must be fielded. The degree of difficulty of the drill is enhanced by varying the speed and the direction of the thrown short hop.

Coaching Points:

- Players should focus on the ball from the time it is thrown to a point where it is all the way into the glove which is then cushioned to the fielder's belt.

- Players should be reminded to keep their feet stationary and rely on moving their knees, hips and hands to catch the short hop thrown directly at them.

- Players should backhand short hops that go to the throwing-hand side and front-hand those balls that are thrown to their glove side.

- Competition in this drill can be achieved by awarding points for properly fielded balls and keeping score.

- The ball should be thrown with a relatively high degree of velocity in order to simulate game conditions.

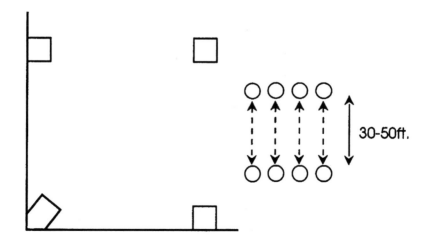

DRILL # 7: BACKHAND FIELDING

Objective: To improve movement mechanics; to practice fielding balls on the throwing-hand side.

Equipment Needed: Gloves and one baseball for every two players.

Description: Working in pairs, the players stand 60 to 75 feet apart facing one another. The drill begins by having one player (A) roll a ground ball to the throwing-hand side of his partner (B). Player B should be forced to backhand the ball. Before each ground ball, the player who will be fielding the ball should assume the proper ready position. As the ground ball is rolled, B should execute a quick crossover step to his throwing-hand side. Upon reaching the ball, player B should firmly plant his throwing foot, go down to the ball by bending his back and legs as appropriate, and put his glove in the proper position to field the ball—open wide and low to the ground. Player B will then focus on the ball until it enters his glove, cushion the ball up and into his waist, and raise up and make a hard, overhand throw to player A without taking a step. Player B should field 10 ground balls and then switch roles with player A.

Coaching Points:

- Players fielding the ball should shove off with their throwing-side leg in order to generate sufficient power in their throws. As a rule, the skip-and-throw technique should not be used because it will take too much time to beat most runners.

- A third player (C) can be incorporated into the drill, by having (C) pitch the ball to (A), who then attempts to hit the ball to the throwing-hand side of (B).

DRILL # 8: PEPPER

Objective: To develop quickness, throwing skills, fielding techniques, and bat-handling ability.

Equipment Needed: Several baseballs, gloves, and a bat.

Description: The drill involves a least two players: one who serves as a hitter (A) and one, two or three who act as fielders (B). The batter and fielder(s) stand approximately 25 feet apart. The drill begins by having the fielder throw (pitch) the ball to the hitter, who attempts to hit the ball back to the fielder using a shortened, controlled swing. Catching the hit ball, the fielder tosses the ball back to the hitter, and the drill continues in a non-stop fashion for a predetermined amount of time or number of swings. Upon reaching that predetermined point, the players rotate.

Coaching Points:

- Hitters should focus on bat control. One way to accomplish this is to require the hitter to hit the ball to a specific spot relative to the player who threw him the ball (hit to the opposite field).

- Fielders should focus on using the proper techniques for fielding the ball and throwing it quickly and accurately.

- While more than two players can engage in this drill (by increasing the number of fielders involved in the drill at any given time), the extra fielders reduce the amount of fielding that any one player actually gets within a specific period of time. No more than three fielders.

- Variety can be added to the drill by having the player who fields a ball hit to him, throw the ball to a designated cutoff player instead of back to the hitter.

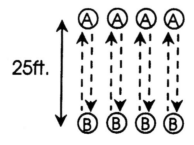

25ft.

DRILL # 9: DROPPED-BALL FIELDING

Objective: To develop fielding and throwing skills. To enhance quickness.

Equipment Needed: One baseball and gloves.

Description: The drill involves two players, using one ball, who are standing approximately 20 to 40 feet apart (depending upon the hypothetical game situation). The drill begins by having a player drop the ball 6 to 8 feet from himself. Once the ball reaches the predetermined distance, the player pounces on the ball, attempts to work on a particular play that he might have on a ground ball during the game (for example, middle infielders might pivot as if they were initiating a double-play, first and third basemen might imagine that they were fielding a bunt), and then throws the ball to his partner. His partner continues the drill by repeating the same sequence of actions. The drill continues for a set period of time or number of plays.

Coaching Points:

- One of the primary keys to the effectiveness of this drill is that the player who drops the ball should explode the ball.

- This drill is an excellent method for warming-up the infielders prior to team infield practice.

- When picking up the ball, the fielder should be careful to use his bare hand and keep his chest directly over the ball.

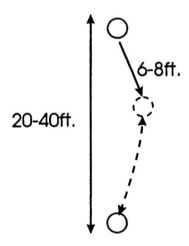

DRILL # 10: WALL BALL

Objective: To improve ball-handling skills and improve reaction time.

Equipment Needed: A wall, and one rubber ball and glove per player.

Description: The drill involves one or more players who are standing approximately 20 to 25 feet from the wall. The drill begins by having each player throw a ball against the wall. Each throw is fielded by the player who made the throw. Variety and difficulty are incorporated into the drill by having the player vary the speed, location, and type of throw. The drill continues for a predetermined number of throws or length of time.

Coaching Points:

- The use of proper fielding techniques should be emphasized at all times.

- The closer a player stands to the wall, the greater the emphasis on quickness.

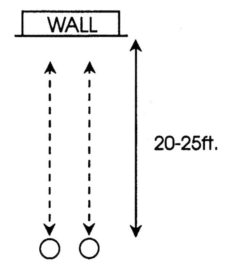

DRILL # 11: LOW THROWS

Objective: To develop the ability to handle low throws and to improve footwork.

Equipment Needed: Gloves, baseballs, and a base.

Description: The drill involves two players standing approximately 30 feet apart. One player is positioned next to a base. The drill begins by having one player throw a ball into the dirt at the other player. That player fields the throw and throws a similar ball back at his partner. Both players concentrate on fielding all types of low throws. The player close to the base tries to keep his foot on the base while fielding the ball as he would during an actual game situation (for example, a first baseman on a low throw, or a middle infielder while fielding a low throw on an attempted steal). After a predetermined number of throws, the players change positions, and the drill continues.

Coaching Points:

- Proper footwork and fielding techniques should be emphasized at all times.

- Variety and difficulty can be incorporated into the drill by varying the speed, location, and type of throw.

- Ball is more important than the bag! If a choice must be made, remove the foot from the bag and be certain to catch or block the ball.

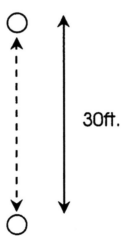

30ft.

DRILL # 12: 3-6-3 DOUBLE PLAY

Objective: To enable first basemen and shortstops to develop the skills and techniques involved in making the 3-6-3 double play.

Equipment Needed: Gloves, several baseballs, and bases.

Description: The first basemen (A) and shortstops (B) form two separate lines: one next to first base and one on the shortstop side of second base. The coach (or the next person in the line of first basemen) stands approximately 25 feet from first base on the home plate side. One of the shortstops (C), acting as a baserunner, is being held on first base by a first baseman. The drill begins by having the coach roll a ball to the first baseman which forces him to come off of the base to field the ball. When the ball leaves the coach's hand, the runner takes off for second. The first baseman fields the ball and initiates the 3-6-3 double play. After a preset number of plays, the players rotate to the end of the line or exchange positions.

Coaching Points:

- Variety can be added to the drill by having the coach vary the location, type, and speed of the ball thrown to the first basemen.

- The drill could initially be conducted without a runner actually being held on.

- The drill could also be conducted with the first baseman playing behind the runner.

- If necessary, early in the season, the distance between the bases can be shortened to minimize arm strain.

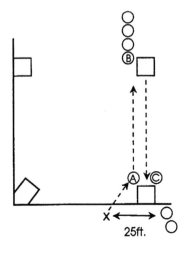

25ft.

DRILL # 13: INFIELDER CUTOFF RELAY

Objective: To develop the skills and techniques involved in making relay throws quickly and accurately.

Equipment Needed: Gloves and baseballs.

Description: Players perform the drill in groups of three. The drill involves the three players formed up in a straight line approximately 60 feet from each other. The drill begins by having the first player in the line throw the ball to the player in the middle of the line. Already having turned his body to his target (the third player in line), the second player catches the throw and quickly throws the ball to the third player. This procedure is designed to simulate the cut-home relay throw. The emphasis should be on both speed and accuracy. After a preset number of throws or minutes, the players should switch positions.

Coaching Points:

- The drill can be varied by placing the three players in a triangle formation instead of a straight line. One player stands near the pitcher's mound, while the other two can be positioned either at first base and second base or at second and third. One player starts the throw by throwing to the player near the mound. After catching the ball, that person has the option of throwing it to the designated base.

- When they're serving as the middle man in a relay, first basemen should learn to catch the ball in the heel of their gloves with two hands, not the webbing.

- Relay men should be reminded to turn their bodies toward their targets and to wave their arms and shout "hit me, hit me" before making the relay throw.

- The players can time each other to see how many throws the middle man can make in a specific amount of time or how quickly he can get off an accurate throw.

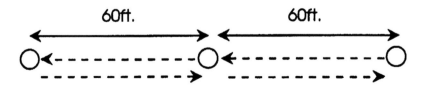

DRILL # 14: POP FLIES

Objective: To develop the skills and techniques involved in fielding pop flies.

Equipment Needed: Fungo bat, gloves, and baseballs.

Description: The drill involves pairs of infielders. Initially, the players throw high pop-ups to each other. One player assumes a ready position and looks straight ahead or down at the ground. His partner throws a high pop-up and yells, "now." The player who must field the ball immediately looks up, locates the ball, moves to it, and catches it. After the players have become relatively adept at his phase of the drill, (they progress to hitting fungo pop flies to each other.) Very few players can handle a fungo that well. It's simply not realistic.

Coaching Points:

- If the sun is out, the coach should always place the infielder in direct line with the sun, so that the infielder practices shading his eyes and making the play.

- This drill should be performed on all types of days—cold, windy, rainy. All factors considered, the tougher the weather, the better.

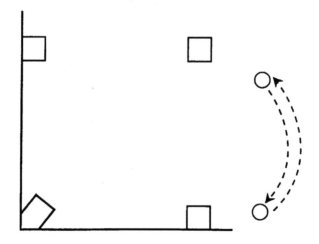

DRILL # 15: CROSS-OVER BASE

Objective: To develop the ability in first basemen to shift to the outside of the bag and tag it while catching a high throw in that direction; to teach the fundamentals involved in shifting, leaving the bag, taking a throw, and tagging a runner.

Equipment Needed: Gloves, baseballs, and a base.

Description: The drill involves two players, a least one of which must be a first baseman. Standing in the infield area approximately 60 feet away, one player throws the ball on the home plate side of first base to the first baseman who adjusts his body position accordingly while either tagging the bag with his foot or a runner with the gloved hand with the ball.

Coaching Points:

- The drill emphasizes good judgment and proper footwork.

- The difficulty of the drill can be increased by varying the type and location of the throw.

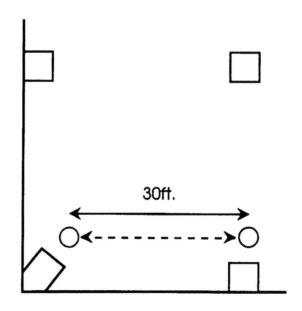

DRILL # 16: THREE PERSON RUNDOWN

Objective: To develop the skills and techniques involved in a rundown play.

Equipment Needed: Gloves, baseballs, and two bases.

Description: The drill involves three players, one acting as a baserunner and two infielders. The coach initiates the drill by throwing the ball to an infielder (A) who is standing next to the base where a baserunner (B) has allowed himself to be picked off. The runner takes off for the next base and attempts to either "steal" the base or avoid the tag as long as possible. The infielder who caught the original throw runs the ball at the baserunner and attempts to force him to continue running toward his partner (C). At the appropriate time, (A) throws the ball to player (C) to make the quick tag. After a preset number of rundowns, the players switch positions.

Coaching Points:

- Tagging the runner out as quickly as possible is emphasized.

- A second baserunner and two more infielders can be added to make the drill go more quickly.

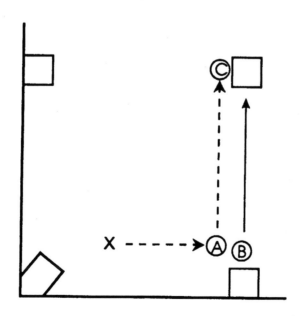

DRILL # 17: THIRD STRIKE THROW TO FIRST

Objective: To teach first basemen the proper way to set up to receive a throw from the catcher on a dropped third strike.

Equipment Needed: Gloves, baseballs, and a base.

Description: The catcher rolls a ball five to 10 feet away from himself, retrieves the ball, and attempts to throw out a phantom runner at first base. The first baseman sets up on the coaches box side of the bag and gives a glove target to the catcher. The first baseman always attempts to give the catcher a good angle to throw at, so that a batter will not be hit in the back by the throw.

Coaching Points:

- The drill could be progressively modified to include an actual baserunner once the basic retrieving-throwing-catching skills are mastered.

- The difficulty of the drill could be increased by having someone other than the catcher roll the ball to be retrieved by the catcher. The location of the throw should then be varied so that the catcher is forced to react to the ball.

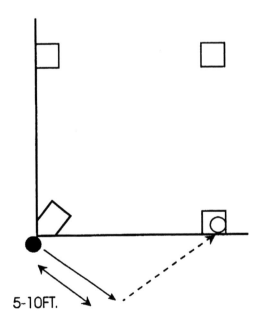

5-10FT.

DRILL # 18: KNEE WALL/FENCE CATCH

Objective: To practice using a short-arm delivery while throwing.

Equipment Needed: Gloves, baseballs, and a wall or fence.

Description: The infielders pair-up. One player (A) kneels with the soles of his feet and his back pressed against a wall or fence. His body is erect. His partner (B) is standing approximately 25 to 30 feet away. Player (A) initiates the drill by rotating his upper body to throw the ball to (B). During the rotation, his hand will hit the wall, forcing him to shorten his backward rotation, and throw the ball from "his ear." Player (B) catches the ball and throws it back to (A). After a predetermined number of throws, the players rotate positions.

Coaching Points:

- Players should concentrate on getting zip on their throws from a kneeling position.

- All throws from a kneeling position should be made quickly.

- The difficulty of the drill can be increased by moving the non-kneeling partner farther away.

- This drill is particularly beneficial for catchers and second basemen who are having trouble mastering a short-arm throwing delivery.

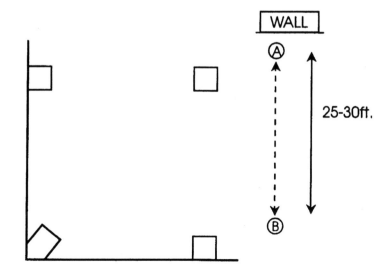

DRILL # 19: BAD HOP

Objective: To practice fielding bad-hop grounders; to develop "soft" hands.

Equipment Needed: Gloves and baseballs.

Description: Players divide into pairs. Each player stands facing his partner who is approximately 15 feet away. The drill involves having each player (A) alternately toss a bad-hop grounder to his partner (B). The partner fields the ball and attempts to throw a bad-hop grounder tack to (A). The drill continues for a preset number of bad-hop grounders being fielded by each player or a preset length of time.

Coaching Points:

- Players should be encouraged to make their throws difficult to field.

- Competition could be conducted between the two players on the basis of fewest misses.

- The drill could also involve practicing tagging an incoming runner. For example, after fielding the bad-hop grounder, the player could be required to execute a swipe tag (to simulate tagging an incoming baserunner).

- The fielder should concentrate on keeping his chest in front of the throw.

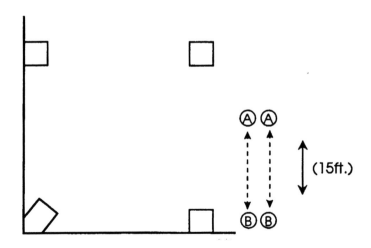

DRILL # 20: DOUBLE PLAY PIVOTS

Objective: To practice double play pivots and throws.

Equipment Needed: Gloves, baseballs, and a fungo bat.

Description: The drill involves all of the infielders. The drill begins by having a coach who is standing approximately 30 to 40 feet in front of home plate in the middle of the diamond to hit or throw a ground ball to a left side infielder (C). The infielder fields the ball and throws it to the second baseman (B) to start the double play. The second baseman makes the pivot and relays the ball to first base (A). After a preset number of plays or length of time, the coach can initiate the drill by hitting or throwing a ground ball to a right-side infielder. The drill continues for a pre- determined length of time.

Coaching Points:

- If the throwing arms of the infielders get tired early in the season, the distance between the bases can be shortened for the drill.

- Proper fielding and throwing techniques should be emphasized at all times.

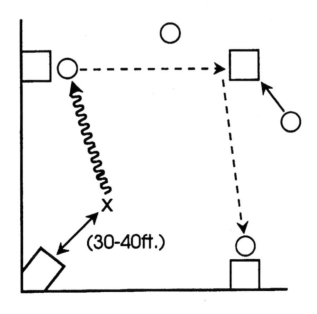

(30-40ft.)

DRILL # 21: PIVOT AND HURDLE THE DUMMY

Objective: To teach middle infielders (shortstops and second basemen) to avoid a sliding runner as they complete the double play.

Equipment Needed: Gloves, baseballs, bases, and a football blocking dummy or a large trash can.

Description: The drill involves having the second basemen (C) and short-stops (B) line up in two separate lines. The shortstops are required to toss the ball (simulating the start of a double play relay) to the first second basemen. That player catches the toss, tags second base, makes the pivot, and relays the ball to first base (A). As the ball is tossed to the player who must then relay it to first base, the coach rolls a blocking dummy at the feet of that player. That player must learn to skip over the dummy as he makes the throw. After each play, the dummy is retrieved by the coach, and the drill continues with the next player in line. After every player in a line has had the opportunity to practice this skill a preset number of times, the two lines switch responsibilities (the tossers become the double play relay throwers and vice-versa).

Coaching Point:

- The player relaying the ball to first must get his shoulders and body turned toward first base as he is throwing in order to minimize his chances of being injured if a collision with the baserunner occurs.

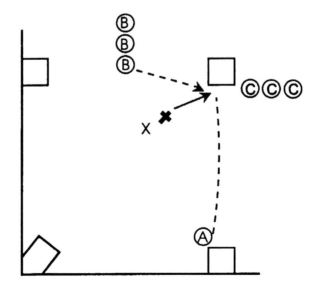

DRILL # 22: SLOW HIT BALLS

Objective: To practice fielding a slowly hit ball and throwing out the runner at first base.

Equipment Needed: Gloves, baseballs, and a fungo bat.

Description: Using a fungo bat, a coach continuously hits slow rollers toward the infielders (third basemen, shortstops, and second basemen). The infielders charge the ball, scoop it into their gloves, and throw out the runner at first base. The drill continues for a preset length of time or number of balls fielded.

Coaching Points:

- Infielders should be reminded to keep their heads down and look the ball into their gloves while fielding.

- The ball should be played with both hands, unless it has almost stopped. In the latter case, the infielder can play it with his bare hand.

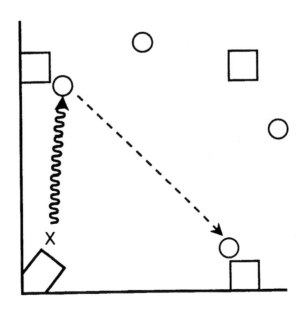

DRILL # 23: PROPER RELAYS

Objective: To teach middle infielders the skills and techniques involved in being an effective relay man.

Equipment Needed: Gloves and baseballs.

Description: The drill involves three infielders in a line, approximately 60 to 70 feet apart from each other. The player in the middle (B) is preferably either a shortstop or a second baseman. Both players on the end of the line (A and C) are facing the middle player. The drill begins by having player A throw the ball to B who is acting as the relay man. Player B catches the ball and relays it to C. Both player A and C simulate tag plays whenever they receive a relay from B. After a preset number of relay throws by B, the three players switch positions.

Coaching Points:

- Players should concentrate on using proper throwing techniques.

- Players serving as the relay man should face the player throwing him the ball, catch the ball with two hands, and then turn and strongly fire the ball to the target.

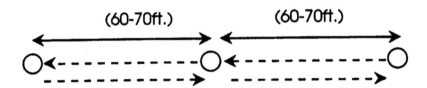

(60-70ft.)   (60-70ft.)

DRILL # 24: 1-4-3 DOUBLE PLAY

Objective: To practice the techniques and footwork involved in a double play which is started by the pitcher.

Equipment Needed: Gloves and baseballs.

Description: The drill involves three players: a pitcher, a middle infielder (alternately a second baseman and a shortstop), and a first baseman. The drill begins by having the pitcher drop a ball at his feet. At that point, the middle infielder breaks for the base with his hands up and shouting, "ball, ball." The pitcher then quickly picks up the ball and throws chest high over the inside corner of the bag to the middle infielder who makes the proper pivot and throws the ball to first base to complete the double play.

Coaching Points:

- The focus is on having both the pitcher and the middle infielder make strong, accurate throws and having the middle infielder use the proper footwork when making the double play pivot.

- Once the basic techniques of the 1-4-3 or the 1-6-3 (depending upon which middle infielder is involved) double play have been mastered, the drill can be made more difficult by either adding a runner at first base or having a coach hit grounders to the pitcher to start the double play.

- If the team's first basemen are working on some other aspect of play (e.g., cover plays, fielding short hops, etc.), an extra pitcher could act as the "first baseman" in the drill. In this instance, the extra pitcher should stand in front of a screen that has been placed $1/_3$ to $1/_2$ of the way up the baseline. The purpose of the screen is to protect teammates who are involved in other drills or exercises.

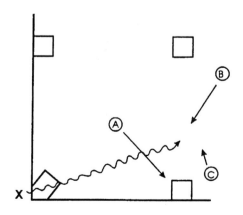

DRILL # 25: FORCE AND TAG PLAYS AT HOME

Objective: To enable infielders to practice fielding ground balls from a drawn-in infield position and throwing out runners at the plate.

Equipment Needed: Gloves, baseballs, and a fungo bat.

Description: The drill involves as many infielders as the coach chooses to use (preferably a full complement of infielders). The infielders assume a position on the lip of the grass. Using a fungo bat, the coach hits ground balls to the infielders who are then required to throw out an imaginary runner at home. The coach calls out the situation, either a "force play" or a "tag play."

Coaching Points:

- On force plays, the infielder should throw a chest-high strike to the catcher. On a tag play, a knee-high throw to the catcher is required.

- The emphasis is on using proper fielding techniques and making quick, strong, and accurate throws.

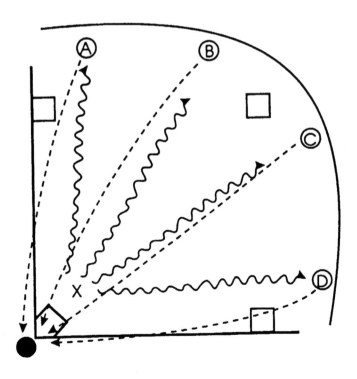

DRILL # 26: SIDE-TO-SIDE

Objective: To develop lateral quickness. To practice fielding techniques while moving laterally.

Equipment Needed: Gloves and baseballs.

Description: The drill involves having the infielders work in pairs. The two players stand approximately 20 feet apart facing each other. One player (A) acts as the hitter, while the other player serves as the fielder (B). The drill begins by having player A roll the ball to B's right or left. Player B moves laterally to field the ball and feigns a throw to a designated base on every ground ball he fields. Player A varies both the location and the relative difficulty of the ground ball he throws to B. Player A tries to get B to extend as far as he can to work on forehand and backhand plays.

Coaching Point:

- The difficulty of the drill can be progressively increased by having the infielder actually throw the ball to first base or by having player A hit grounders (using a fungo bat) to B instead of throwing them.

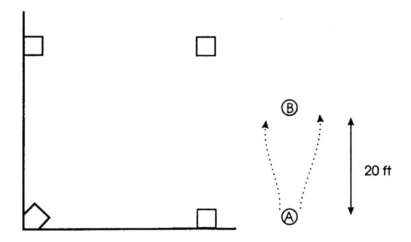

DRILL # 27: POP UPS

Objective: To practice fielding pop flies.

Equipment Needed: Gloves, baseballs, and a fungo bat.

Description: The drill involves as many infielders as the coach chooses to use (preferably a full complement of infielders). The drill entails having a coach hit fungo pop flies to various locations and having the infielders practice fielding the pop-ups. The pop flies are hit to each of the locations the infielders might have to deal with during the game: short left field, short center field, short right field, on the field, and in foul territory.

Coaching Points:

- More than one fungo hitter can be used at a time to increase the number of pop flies which must be handled.

- Whenever possible, the drill should be performed on a sunny day to enable the infielder to practice not losing the ball in the sun.

- Verbal communication is essential to this drill, as is the understanding of which fielder has priority depending upon where the ball is descending.

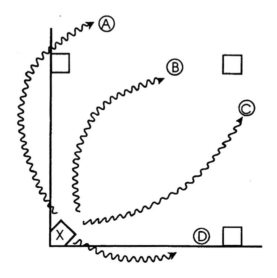

DRILL # 28: FIRST AND THIRD

Objective: To practice defending against the first-and-third, no-out situation; to provide an indoor activity during inclement weather.

Equipment Needed: Gloves, moveable rubber bases, tennis balls, and a bat.

Description: The drill involves two teams of infielders with six infielders per team: catcher, pitcher, first baseman, second baseman, third baseman, and shortstop. Catchers wear a mask. The game is played with a tennis ball. Team #1 takes the field. Team #2 positions runners at first and third and has a batter at the plate. The tactical situation is runners at first and third with no outs. The catcher (or the coach) serves as the umpire. The batter must use a choke grip while swinging. The batter is given two strikes to advance the runners. He may not walk or receive a base as a result of being hit by the pitch. In addition, he is out if he hits the ball over the infield or fouls off a pitch when he already has one strike. He can bunt, take a first strike, or foul off a first strike. If he makes contact with the ball and hits a grounder, the situation is live. The batter runs to first base and the baserunners attempt to advance. If the batter makes an out, the next player in line becomes the hitter. After three outs, the teams change sides: team #2 takes the field, and team #1 is at the plate. The team that scores the most runs wins.

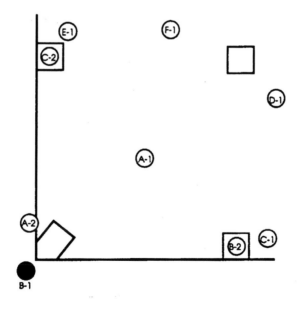

DRILL # 29: POP-THE-TARGET

Objective: To practice the techniques and skills involved in fielding a ball while on the run and making a strong accurate throw to first base; to provide an indoor activity during inclement weather.

Equipment Needed: Gloves, a moveable rubber base, and rubber or soft balls.

Description: A target area, measuring three-by-one foot, is taped onto a gymnasium wall approximately three feet above the floor. The drill involves three players at a time and a coach who stands to one side of the target area and judges all thrown balls. A rubber base is placed about 100 feet in front of the wall to serve as a point of reference. One player (A) assumes a position adjacent to the base, approximately 50 feet to the right of the target. A second player (B) stands (out of the line of the throw) next to the target area and retrieves balls thrown at the target. A third player (C), standing 50 to 60 feet in front of A, is responsible for rolling ground balls to A which he must field. Player C can either roll the ball or throw a slow bouncing ground ball. Player A must charge the ball, field it, get set, and throw at the target area as quickly as possible. Points are awarded to player A on how well he fields and throws the ball: three points for a cleanly fielded ball thrown into the target area, two points for a cleanly fielded ball which hits the edge of the target, one point for a cleanly fielded ball which misses the target, and no points for a misfielded ball.

Coaching Points:

- Players should stay low while fielding and keep their eyes on the ball.

- Players should be reminded of the need to set before throwing. Throws made off plays performed in one swooping motion are often wild.

- Point competition between players can be conducted with this drill.

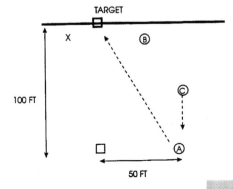

CHAPTER 2

OUTFIELDER DRILLS

DRILL # 30: ON YOUR TOES

Objective: To develop the ability to pick up the flight of the ball; to teach outfielders to break on the ball with good vision when running after a fly ball.

Equipment Needed: Baseballs and gloves.

Description: The outfielders line up outside the right foul line facing the infield. On command from the coach, the first player in line sprints to his right and catches a ball thrown by his coach. He then runs back to his left to catch another ball thrown by the coach. Next, he immediately sprints to his right again to catch a third ball thrown by his coach. After catching each thrown ball, the player tosses it back to the coach. After the third ball is thrown (and caught), the player returns to the end of the line. The next player in line steps up, and the drill continues.

Coaching Points:

- Players should run on their toes, not on their heels.
- Players should select and focus on a head-high point while running before they turn to look for a thrown ball.
- Players should look for a thrown ball by turning their heads, not their entire bodies.
- In order to protect the throwing arm of the coach, the still can involve having the coach hit (fungo) the ball to the outfielders instead of throwing it.
- Variety can be added to the drill by dividing the outfielders into either two or three equal-sized groups. If two groups are formed, one group (A) can field the hit or thrown ball. Once (A) fields the ball, he quickly throws the ball back in to the other group (B). If the third group (C) is involved, that group assumes the roll of the coach by either throwing or hitting the ball to (A) to initiate the drill.
- This drill can also serve as an excellent conditioning exercise.

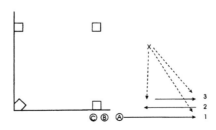

DRILL # 31: CATCH IT IF YOU CAN

Objective: To develop and improve fielding techniques and fundamentals of outfielding.

Equipment Needed: Baseball, gloves, and a bat.

Description: The drill involves a coach who hits a variety of ground balls and fly balls to players who are positioned in the outfield. In addition, one player is designated as a cutoff (relay) player. After fielding a ball hit by the coach, the player catching the ball throws it to the relay man, who in turn throws it to a player who is serving as a catcher to feed balls to the coach (as needed). Standing on the right field foul line approximately 25 to 30 feet beyond first base, the coach hits balls on a fairly continuous basis. After fielding a ball, the outfielder immediately assumes the ready position again. Once an outfielder has fielded a specific number of balls, a new outfielder rotates into the drill. The player being replaced then either goes to the end of the line or substitutes for either the relay man or the catcher.

Coaching Points:

- The drill can be performed with one or more outfielders at a time.
- The coach can vary the location, speed, and type of ball hit.
- Players should be required to make good throws to the cutoff man.
- Also serves as an excellent conditioning drill.

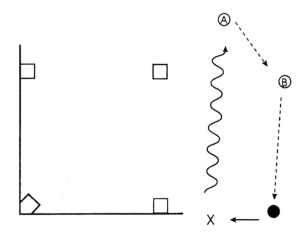

DRILL # 32: BALLS AT THE FENCE

Objective: To develop the skills and techniques required to play a ball which is lying next to a fence.

Equipment Needed: Four baseballs per threesome, gloves, and a fence.

Description: The drill involves three players, two of whom act as outfielders, while one serves as a cutoff (relay) man. Four balls are placed next to a fence about five feet apart from each other. The two outfielders line up about 25 feet from the fence, while the cutoff man is approximately 75 feet from the fence. The drill commences by having the first man in line sprint to one of the balls and pick it up. Right-handed outfielders should pick up the ball with the bare hand, with their right foot positioned to the right of the ball without straddling the ball but with his chest over the ball. Left-handed outfielders should position themselves with the left foot to the left of the ball. Upon picking up the ball, a player should begin his throw as quickly as possible at precisely the point where he picked up the ball. After throwing the ball to the cutoff man, the player returns to the starting area. The second outfielder then continues the drill by running to pick up the next ball. After the four balls have been picked up and thrown, the players rotate, and the drill starts over.

Coaching Points:

- Players should be reminded that because the average runner takes four to five strides per second, time is of the essence when initiating a throw.
- More than one group of outfielders can perform the drill simultaneously.

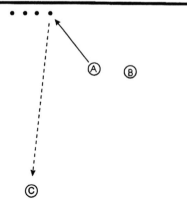

DRILL # 33: FIVE PLAYER RELAY

Objective: To develop the skills and techniques required to make relay throws quickly and precisely.

Equipment Needed: Baseballs and gloves.

Description: Players work in groups of five. Depending on the age of the players, the players line up in relatively straight lines, approximately 60 to 70 feet apart from each other. The drill begins by having the first player in line make a strong, accurate throw to the second player. The second player then makes a similar throw to the third player, and so forth. Once the ball has been thrown to the last player in line, the drill is repeated in the opposite direction. All players should be taught to adjust their body positions while the ball is in flight so that they are able to simply catch the ball and throw it immediately with maximum velocity and accuracy regardless of the thrown ball's path as it approaches them.

Coaching Points:

- The proper techniques for throwing should be emphasized.
- Each cycle of the drill can be timed to set a standard of relative comparison.
- Competition can be staged against two or more groups performing the drill simultaneously.

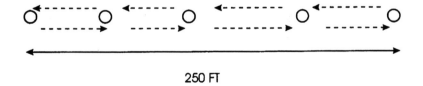

250 FT

DRILL # 34: EVER LONGER CATCH

Objective: To develop arm strength for throwing and to practice long, accurate throws.

Equipment Needed: Baseballs and gloves.

Description: Working in pairs, the outfielders start approximately 75 feet apart and gradually increase the distance between each other to 200 feet. Beginning at 75 feet and continuing every five feet or so, the players throw the ball to each other. The emphasis is on making a long, accurate throw. The ball should be thrown chest high to a player's partner. To get his body's momentum and force behind his throw, a player should crow hop before releasing the ball.

Coaching Points:

- To add variety to the drill, a player could intentionally drop the ball in front of himself after catching it and then scramble after it, before making a return throw to his partner.
- The distance between the players can be decreased if any of several factors suggest that such an action would be appropriate: it's early in the season, the players involved are relatively young, or if one of the players has a sore arm.

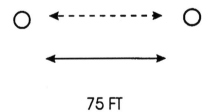

75 FT

DRILL # 35: FIELD LIKE A SHORTSTOP

Objective: To practice fielding ground balls. To improve the ability of an outfielder to throw accurately to a base.

Equipment Needed: Gloves and baseballs.

Description: Working in pairs, the outfielders stand approximately 120 feet apart. One player, serving as a first baseman (A), rolls (throws) the ball to his partner (B). Player B charges the ground ball, fields it like a shortstop, and makes a strong, accurate throw to A (who is hypothetically the cutoff man at the plate). After a preset number of fielding chances, the players switch roles.

Coaching Points:

- Using proper fielding techniques and making a strong, accurate throw should be emphasized.
- Outfielders should be reminded of their need to be able to field ground balls well and to be able to quickly throw to a specific target.

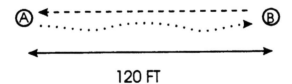

120 FT

DRILL # 36: BODY BLOCK GROUND BALLS

Objective: To practice using the body to block ground balls. To teach outfielders not to let bad hop grounders get by them in the outfield. To improve the ability to scramble after a ball which has been blocked.

Equipment Needed: Gloves and baseballs.

Description: Working in pairs, the outfielders stand 60 to 70 feet apart. The drill involves having one player (A) throw a hard ground ball at his partner (B). Player B moves to the ball, gets in front of it, drops his throwing side knee to the ground, protects his groin area with his glove hand, and uses his body to block the ball to keep it from getting past him. Once the ball has been blocked, player B quickly picks it up and uses his kneeling leg to vault himself into a standing position. Player B then makes a strong, accurate throw to A. After a preset number of repetitions, the players switch roles.

Coaching Points:

- The drills can be made more difficult by varying the location and speed of the ground balls which are thrown by player A.
- The need to get squarely in front of balls to be blocked should be emphasized.

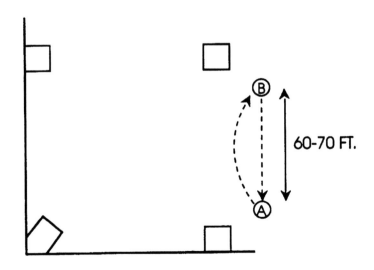

DRILL # 37: CUTOFF RELAY

Objective: To practice hitting the cutoff man with a strong, chest-high throw.

Equipment Needed: Gloves and baseballs.

Description: Working in pairs, the outfielders stand approximately 150 feet apart. Player (A) flips the ball behind himself, turns and races for the ball, picks it up, wheels to his glove-hand side, and throws a chest-high strike to his partner (B). Player B catches the ball and continues the drill by performing the actions of A in the same order. The drill continues for a preset number of repetitions.

Coaching Points:

- The emphasis should be on quickly getting to and picking up the ball with the bare hand and the chest over the ball, and making a strong, accurate throw.
- Variety (and an increased level of difficulty) can be added to the drill by having either a third player or the coach flip the ball to be picked up instead of by player A. In that instance, player A must also learn to locate the ball quickly.

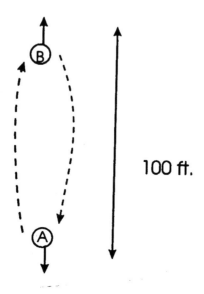

DRILL # 38: SLIDING CATCHES

Objective: To practice catching a fly ball while sliding. To develop the ability to make low or shoestring catches.

Equipment Needed: Gloves and baseballs.

Description: The drill can be performed either outdoors on the outfield grass or indoors in the gymnasium. Long pants should be worn by those players participating in the drill. Working in pairs, the outfielders line up approximately 60 to 70 feet from each other. One player (A) lobs a short fly ball to his partner (B), who races in, slides feet first toward the infield, and attempts to catch the ball on the fly alongside his body while sliding. After a preset number of repetitions, the players switch roles.

Coaching Points:

- Players must learn to accurately judge the flight of the ball and to time their slide accordingly.
- Players should focus on the ball at all times.
- The difficulty of the drill can be increased by varying the location and speed of the lobbed fly ball or my moving the outfielders further apart to make the distance player B must cover greater.

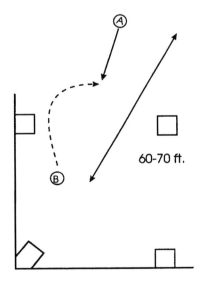

DRILL # 39: IN THE ALLEY

Objective: To teach outfielders to coordinate responsibilities on ground balls and fly balls that are hit between them in the alleys (gaps).

Equipment Needed: Gloves and baseballs.

Description: The drill involves two players and a coach. (Note: A third player could perform the duties of the coach in this drill.) One player (A) is positioned in center field, while the other player (B) serves as the flank (right fielder or left fielder) outfielder. The coach throws or hits a ball between players A and B, who must then coordinate who should make the play. The general rule of thumb on all balls hit into the gap, ground or fly balls, is that the flank outfielder will pass in front of the center fielder in making the play. As a result, flank outfielders usually will play line drives hit in the alley which are above waist high because they are passing in front. Center fielders, on the other hand, make the plays on low catches because they are taking a deeper angle to the ball. On high fly balls hit in the gap, the center fielder usually calls off the flank outfielder. In this instance, an exception is made if it is a throwing play and the flank outfielder has a stronger throwing arm.

Coaching Points:

- The drill can be expanded to include both flank outfielders and the center fielder at the same time.
- Players fielding the ball initially lob the ball back to the coach. Once the basic skills of the drill have been mastered, the fielder can be required to make a strong throw to a specific target.
- Verbal communication between the two outfielders is essential. The centerfielder has priority over the flank outfielders.

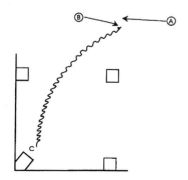

DRILL # 40: COORDINATING POP-UPS

Objective: To enable outfielders and infielders to practice coordinating their "calls" and responsibilities on pop flies that are hit between the two groups.

Equipment Needed: Fungo bat, gloves and baseballs.

Description: The drill involves a pre-selected group of players: the right side of play (the first baseman, the second baseman, and the right fielder), the left side (the third baseman, the shortstop, and the left fielder), or the middle of the playing area (the shortstop, the second baseman, and the center fielder). The drill is initiated by having a fungo hitter hit pop flies into the short outfield area. The players participating in the drill are then responsible for coordinating between themselves regarding who must make the play. The outfielder has the priority on the "call" and must make a decision no later than his fourth stride as to whether he is going to take the play or call an infielder onto the ball. Priority rules for coordinating on "tweener" pop flies must be established and followed.

Coaching Points:

- The key is the incoming outfielder reaching a decision as early as possible and yelling, "I've got it" or "you've got it."
- An early call by the outfielder can help prevent a collision (and the resulting injuries) between players.

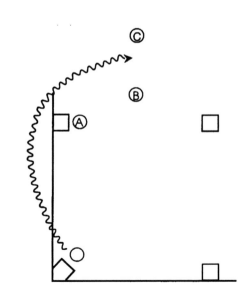

DRILL # 41: OFF THE WALL

Objective: To practice playing balls which have been hit close to or off the outfield fence. To develop a "feel" for the fence (wall).

Equipment Needed: Gloves, baseballs, and a fungo bat.

Description: Initially, the drill involves having a coach hit fungo fly balls next to the fence. The outfielders (one at a time) race back and try to make the proper play. They key for an outfielder is to always get to the fence as quickly as he can, find it by feeling for it with his throwing hand, and prepare to make the play with his glove hand. Once the outfielders have mastered the basic techniques involved in the drill to this point, the coach can then expand the drill by hitting the ball against the fence in addition to adjacent to the fence. Whenever this occurs, the outfielders should play the ball off the fence and be prepared to throw the ball to the relay man.

Coaching Points:

- The coach should vary the location and type of ball he hits.
- The drill can also involve more than one outfielder at a time so that they can also work on coordinating the balls hit to or near the fence in the gap.

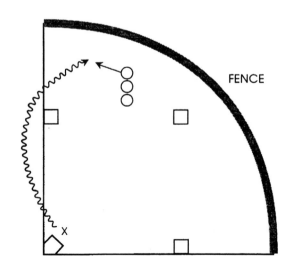

DRILL # 42: ONE LOOK IS ENOUGH

Objective: To develop the ability in an outfielder to hear the crack of the ball on the bat, take one look, race to the point where he thinks the ball will be, and make the catch.

Equipment Needed: Gloves, baseballs, and a fungo bat.

Description: The drill involves a fungo hitter and an outfielder. The fungo hitter calls out "ready" to the outfielder. Upon hearing the "ready" call, the outfielder resumes his outfield stance and looks at the ground. The fungo hitter then hits the ball. As soon as the outfielder hears the ball hit the bat, he gets one quick look to find the ball. He must then race to the spot where he thinks the ball will come down and make the play. Several stations (each with one hitter and one outfielder) can perform the drill simultaneously.

Coaching Points:

- The fungo hitter should vary the location and type of ball hit.
- The outfielder is only allowed "one brief look."
- The ball can also be thrown as another player hits two bats together.

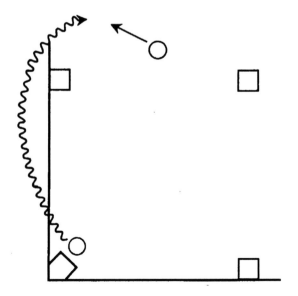

DRILL # 43: LINE DRIVE

Objective: To practice fielding line drives. To improve an outfielder's ability to properly judge line drives which are hit directly at him.

Equipment Needed: Gloves, baseballs, and a fungo bat.

Description: The drill involves one to three outfielders who are required to field line drives which are hit directly at them by the coach. Using a fungo bat, the coach hits a continuous series of head-high drives at the outfielders who must judge the ball and make the play. The outfielders are positioned 150 to 175 feet from the fungo hitter.

Coaching Points:

- Outfielders must learn to judge whether a line drive will sink, or break to the left or right.
- The coach should vary the location and the type of line drives he hits.
- When the ball is hit, the outfielder should drop slightly in order to create a better vision line (angle) to track the ball and to get to where the ball is going to land.

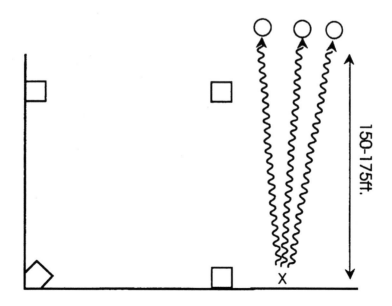

DRILL # 44: ONE-HOP THROWS

Objective: To practice making accurate, single-bounce throws to the bases.

Equipment Needed: Baseballs, gloves, bases, and a fungo bat.

Description: The drill involves having the coach hit fungo fly balls to outfielders who are in a deep outfield position. The outfielders field the ball and then make a strong, one-hop throw to the base designated by the coach (initially second base, then third base, and finally home plate). The outfielders concentrate on making accurate single-bounce, line drive throws.

Coaching Points:

- Competition between the outfielders can be conducted by awarding points for the accuracy of the throw: two points for a one-bounce accurate throw and one point for an accurate throw which either doesn't bounce before getting to the base or bounces more than once, and no points for an inaccurate throw.
- To add variety to the drill, the fungo hitter can vary the location and the type of ball hit to the outfielders; baserunners could also be employed in the drill to simulate "live" action.
- A cutoff man can be stationed in line with the base and the outfielder's throw to serve as a target.

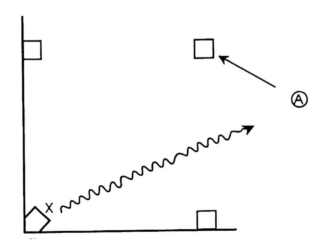

DRILL # 45: FOCUS ON THE CROSS SEAM

Objective: To practice throwing using a cross seam grip.

Equipment Needed: Gloves and baseballs.

Description: Working in pairs, the outfielders start the drill by standing facing each other approximately 60 feet apart. They take turns throwing to each other using a cross seam grip. They should apply the cross seam grip without looking at the ball and should concentrate on completely following through on each throw. The drill continues by having the partners slowly move apart by stepping backward. Every few steps, they throw to each other. Once they have reached a point where they are approximately 150 feet apart, they make one-bounce throws to each other. Still using a cross seam grip, each player throws the ball approximately 15-18 feet in front of his partner. A cross seam grip will ensure that the ball will follow a direct path in flight and after bouncing. Once the players are approximately 250 feet apart, either the drill can be started over or a third player can be added to serve as a cutoff man.

Coaching Points:

- All throws should be free of sideward motion.
- A cross seam grip will prevent a ball from curving, twisting, or sliding.

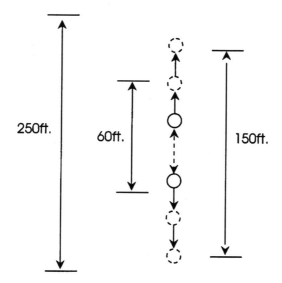

DRILL # 46: MOVING UP

Objective: To practice catching a fly ball while running forward. To develop stamina.

Equipment Needed: Gloves and baseballs.

Description: The drill involves outfielders working in pairs. One player (A) acts as a tosser, while his partner (B) is the fielder. Both players start the drill by standing facing each other approximately 150 feet apart. Player A initiates the drill by tossing a fly ball approximately 130 feet to B who must run up to catch the ball. After catching or retrieving the ball, player B throws the ball back to A and then sprints back to his original position. The drill continues in the same sequence with player A tossing the ball to B. Each subsequent toss, however, is shorter to require player B to run further and faster each time. Once the toss is only about 50 feet, the players switch roles.

Coaching Points:

- Player B should assume a proper ready stance before each tossed ball.
- This drill is excellent for early season conditioning and can also be conducted indoors during inclement weather.

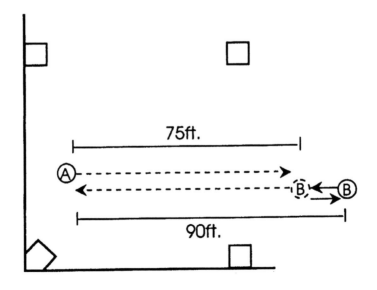

DRILL # 47: OVER-THE-SHOULDER CATCH

Objective: To practice catching a fly ball over the shoulder.

Equipment Needed: Gloves and baseballs.

Description: Every player is given a ball and is assigned to a line. Each line has a tosser, who begins the drill by standing to the left of the line. The first player (A) in line hands his baseball to the tosser and then sprints straight out under control. The tosser then throws a fly ball over player A's head so A must reach to catch the ball over his left shoulder. After catching or retrieving the ball, player A jogs back to the end of the line. The next player in line hands his ball to the tosser, and the drill continues.

Coaching Points:

- Variety can be added to the drill by having the tosser stand to the right of the line and throw the ball over the players' right shoulders.
- The key is to develop the ability to properly judge the path and speed of the thrown ball.

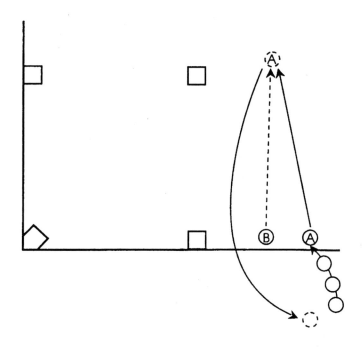

DRILL # 48: GOTCHA

Objective: To practice fielding balls hit directly at a player. To practice making accurate throws. To provide an inclement weather activity.

Equipment Needed: Gloves and rubber or soft baseballs.

Description: The outfielders divide into two groups of three to four players each. If a team has more than eight outfielders, the number of groups or the size of each group can be increased. Remaining several feet apart, the two groups line up facing the gymnasium wall approximately 30 feet from the wall. A strip of tape should be placed at eye level on the wall to serve as a target. One player from each group participates in the drill at a time. The drill begins by having the first player in line one (A) throw a ball at the tape on the wall. The first player in the other line (B) then plays the ball thrown off the wall. Both players receive points for accuracy and proficiency. Player A gets two points for a throw which hits the tape, one point for a throw within six inches of the tape, zero points for throws landing further than six inches from the tape, and minus one point for throws which do not come directly back at the two groups after hitting the wall. Player B gets two points for catching the ball on the fly off the wall, one point for fielding a single-bounce ball, zero points for fielding balls which bounce more than once, and minus one point for making an error or failing to field a ball judged as catchable. After the play, each player goes to the end of the other group's line. The drill continues as before. The first team to score a preset number of points wins.

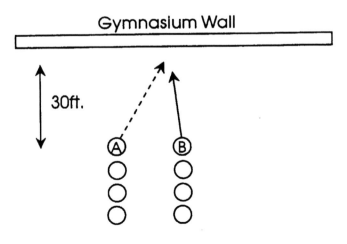

Gymnasium Wall

30ft.

(A) (B)

DRILL # 49: PIN POINT THROWS

Objective: To practice making accurate throws. To practice fielding and provide for an inclement weather activity.

Equipment Needed: Gloves and soft rubber baseballs.

Description: The drill involves having the outfielders forming a single line approximately 100 feet from and facing the gymnasium wall. A target area is taped on the wall. The target should be located approximately two feet from the gymnasium floor and be three feet long by two feet high. The coach stands in front of the target and serves as the judge of all throws. The first player in line (A) stands 40 feet in front of the coach and serves as the cutoff man. The next player in line (B) must field the ball tossed to him. The drill begins by having player A toss a ground ball or a fly ball to B. Player B then fields the ball and throws it on a line at the target to A. Player A lines up between the coach and B. Player B concentrates on throwing the ball shoulder high and to the glove side of A. Player B attempts to make a throw which bounces only once before hitting the target. If the throw is off-line, the coach yells, "cut," and player A catches the throw. If the coach remains silent, the throw is allowed to go through to the wall. Points are awarded for the accuracy of player B's throw: two points for hitting the target squarely, one point for hitting the border of the target, and zero points for off-target throws. After two throws, the players rotate: player A goes to the end of the line, and player B becomes the cutoff man. The first player to earn a preset number of points wins.

Coaching Points:

- A shoulder-high, glove-side throw to the cutoff man makes it easier to handle the throw.
- Power can be added to the throw by using an overhand motion with a complete follow through while throwing.

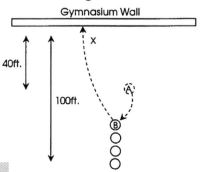

59

CHAPTER 3

CATCHER DRILLS

DRILL # 50: GIVING SIGNS

Objective: To ensure that the catchers and the entire pitching staff fully understand the signs that the catchers will be using during a game.

Equipment Needed: Full catching gear for all catchers (optional).

Description: The drill involves all of the catchers and the pitchers on the team. The pitchers are spread out across the pitching mound area, reading the signs given by the catcher. The catchers form a line. The first catcher in line assumes his catching position behind home plate and gives a varying series of ten signs: pitches, pick offs, first and third signs, and pitch locations. The pitchers collectively read the signs, ensure that they were given clearly, and reach an agreement regarding their universal meaning. After giving the signs, the catcher moves to the end of the line. The next catcher in line takes his place, and the drill continues.

Coaching Points:

- This drill is particularly valuable when conducted before the season begins.
- This drill can be performed either indoors or outdoors.
- It is helpful to have the shortstop and second baseman included with the pitchers.

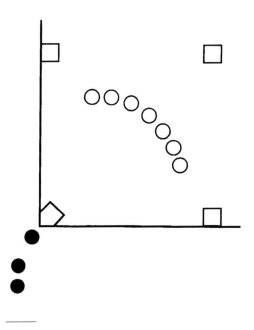

DRILL # 51: GIVING COMMANDS

Objective: To ensure that the catcher is cognizant of his many responsibilities behind home plate during the game; to practice using the proper verbal commands attendant to specific situations.

Equipment Needed: Full catching gear and gloves.

Description: The drill involves the entire infield. The drill begins by having the coach give the "game situation." The catcher then calls out the commands concerning the situation at hand. For example, in a bunt situation, the catcher calls out bunt defenses; on ground balls hit to the right side, he calls out a predetermined signal, such as "cover" or "get over there," to remind the pitcher to cover first base; when a baserunner is on third base, he sets the infield depths; on plays to the outfield, he lines up the relay men and calls out the relay commands; and during the course of the game, he is often asked to place the outfielders in their proper positions.

Coaching Points:

- This drill can be performed either indoors or outdoors.
- The catcher should be reminded that he has a leadership role during the game. He must get his defense in the right place at the right time.

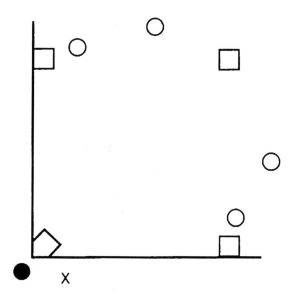

DRILL # 52: CATCH LIKE A CATCHER

Objective: To teach catchers to act, throw, and receive like catchers the moment they step onto the field.

Equipment Needed: Two catchers in full catcher's gear and a baseball.

Description: The players play catch with each other, starting 60 feet apart and working back to 100 feet. They should catch the ball in a semi-crouched position (athletic position), getting their bodies and gloves behind each throw. They should use a short-arm throw to return the ball to their partner. This method of playing catch is designed to greatly improve the skills and techniques involved in both catching and throwing.

Coaching Points:

- Catchers should focus on quickly transferring the ball from their glove hand to their throwing hand, while they are torquing their upper bodies to throw (load position).
- Catchers should employ the quick, short-arm method of throwing.
- Like pitchers, catchers also "load and explode" while throwing.
- Like pitchers, catchers should keep their glove hands tucked when they throw to second base to get runners trying to steal. When catchers are having trouble throwing accurately, it is usually because of lead arm or glove hand problems.
- A device, such as a Gillespie Hitting and Pitching Vest, can be worn by catchers when engaged in drills which involve throwing to remind them to keep their front sides closed. This drill should constantly reemphasize to the players to play "catch like a catcher."

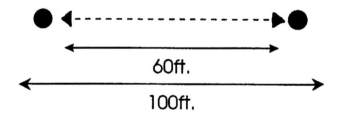

DRILL # 53: SELF CATCH AND BALL TRANSFER

Objective: To improve the ability of a catcher to quickly get the ball to the "load or trigger" position; to develop the kinesthetic sense for turning the ball to grip it across the seams; to practice the techniques involved in assuming the proper position for throwing.

Equipment Needed: One baseball glove per player.

Description: The drill involves having a player repeatedly fire the ball into his glove, bring the ball out of the glove, and move into a throwing position with proper grip on the ball as quickly as possible. This drill is a very important exercise for enabling a catcher to get the "feel" of a baseball and practice the mechanics of getting into the proper position for throwing as quickly as possible.

DRILL # 54: SHIFT DRILL—NO HANDS

Objective: To help catchers learn to shift on pitches in the dirt and to block the ball with their bodies while keeping their hands behind their backs, sliding right or left, and never letting the ball get past them. To develop lateral quickness by working the abductor and adductor thigh muscles.

Equipment Needed: Full catching equipment, several baseballs, and a home plate.

Description: The drill involves players working in pairs: one as a receiver and one as a thrower. The receiving catcher gets behind the plate in a receiving stance, tucks his hands behind his back, blocks balls thrown into the dirt to his right and left, and attempts to funnel blocked balls back toward home plate. The thrower throws fairly hard one-hoppers from a distance of approximately 25 feet from the plate. After 15 throws, the players exchange positions. The drill continues for a preset number of blocked throws.

Coaching Points:

- The key is to have the receiving catcher get squarely behind the ball with his body angled toward home plate in order to funnel all balls back to the plate.
- The catchers should be taught to react first with their bodies and not their hands. They should cushion the ball and catch it with their bodies. Once they conceive of this idea, blocking will become easier and surer.
- Catchers can also perform this drill alone, without equipment, by imagining a pitch coming at them in the dirt and blocking the imaginary ball.
- The drill can be performed progressively by having the throwing catcher initially call out the location of his throws and subsequently require the receiver to be ready to go any direction.

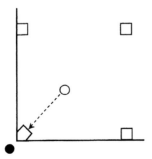

DRILL # 55: SHIFT DRILL—WITH HANDS

Objective: To help catchers learn how to use their bodies and their hands to block throws and pitches; to practice proper footwork for shifting; to develop lateral quickness by working the abductor and the adductor muscles.

Equipment Needed: Full catching gear, baseballs, and a home plate.

Description: The procedures for conducting this drill are exactly the same as for the preceding drill, with the exception of the fact that in this drill catchers should use their gloves and bodies to block the ball. Their hands should be used to protect their groin area and block the opening that might otherwise exist in the groin area. They should not try to catch the ball with their hands. Their chin should be in a tucked position (pressed downward towards their throat) to protect their Adam's apple. After a preset number of repetitions, the players rotate positions.

Coaching Points:

- Catchers should attempt to catch the ball with their belly button and chest and knock it back toward home plate.
- This drill should be mastered to the point that it is instinctive.
- Catchers should concentrate on "block, don't catch."

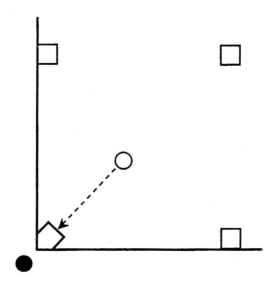

DRILL # 56: BLOCK AND SCRAMBLE AND THROW

Objective: To practice blocking a wild pitch in the dirt, scrambling after the ball, and throwing a baserunner out at second base.

Equipment Needed: Full catching gear, baseballs, and gloves.

Description: The procedures for conducting this drill are the same as for the preceding drill, with a few exceptions. In this drill, the catcher must scramble for the ball after he blocks it and quickly throw it to second base. An extra player is needed to catch the throws to second base (A). Depending on the number of players available, another player could be incorporated into the drill to serve as a baserunner attempting to take second base on the blocked ball. After a preset number of plays, the players switch positions.

Coaching Points:

- If extra players are available, variety could be added to the drill by incorporating another baserunner (this one at second base) and two more infielders: a first baseman and a third baseman. The catcher could then throw to any base (to catch runners off base or to catch a runner stealing third).
- The drill should be conducted with minimal rest: the players should be kept working at all times.
- After blocking, the catcher must get his chest over the ball and pick up the ball with his bare hand.

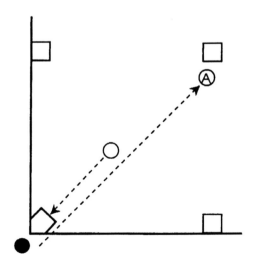

DRILL # 57: GOALIE

Objective: To practice blocking skills; to improve reaction time; to foster competition.

Equipment Needed: Full catching gear and two goals (hockey nets).

Description: Two goals are set up approximately five feet apart. The catcher assumes a ready (catching) position between the goals. Another player (or the coach) stands facing the catcher 40 to 50 feet directly in front of the goals. The objective of the game is to have the player in front of the catcher attempt to throw a ball, which must hit the dirt in front of the net to count, into the nets. The catcher attempts to keep the throw from the nets. One point is earned for either each successful block or each throw into the net. Either a preset number of plays or a present number of earned points constitutes a game.

Coaching Points:

- Variety can be added to the drill by having the catcher scramble after each blocked ball.
- The player attempting to throw the ball into the net should vary his throws (location and intensity).
- It is best to perform this drill at home plate on a dirt surface.

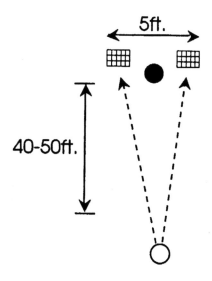

DRILL # 58: ON THE BUTTON

Objective: To practice making quick, accurate throws to each base.

Equipment Needed: Full catching gear, baseballs, and gloves.

Description: The drill involves three players: a catcher (A), and a player (B), usually another catcher, who serves as the infielder who covers the base, and a player (C) who acts as the pitcher. In some instances, a coach may decide to act as the pitcher. The drill is initiated by having player C, who is standing approximately 25 feet in front of A, throw (pitch) the ball to A. From a ready position stand, player A receives the "pitch" and fires it to B at first base. After 10 throws to first base, player B moves to the next base. Player A then throws 10 times to second base. The same scenario is then repeated at third base. Before the three players switch positions, the entire sequence is repeated, five throws to each of the three bases, for a total of 45 throws by player A.

Coaching Points:

- The drill can be performed without a pitcher (C). Player A simply feigns receiving a pitch and then fires to B who is standing 90 feet away.
- Using proper throwing mechanics should be emphasized at all times.

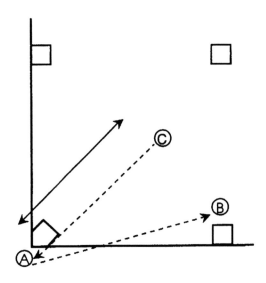

DRILL # 59: DUGOUT GOALIE

Objective: To practice keeping overthrown balls from going into the first base dugout area; to emphasize the importance of preventing the ball from leaving the playing area.

Equipment Needed: Full catching gear, baseballs, gloves, and two red cones.

Description: The drill involves two catchers: a player (A) is serving as the catcher and a player (B) who tosses the ball to A to retrieve. A hypothetical tactical situation is established where a ground ball has been hit with no runners on base. Two red cones are placed five to 10 feet apart, approximately 40 feet from player A, to designate the "dugout area." The drill begins by having player B yell, "now" and then rolls the ball to the dugout (in red cones). On the call, player A breaks on a 45-degree angle for the dugout in an attempt to keep the ball from "getting into" the dugout. By protecting the dugout, A helps prevent a baserunner from advancing to second base. After a preset number of plays, the players switch roles.

Coaching Points:

- If necessary, the distance that player A has to run to the dugout can be shortened.
- The drill can be expanded by having player A scramble to his feet after retrieving the ball thrown by B and throw a strike toward second base (to player B).

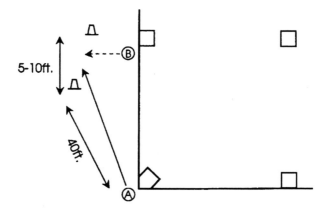

DRILL # 60: FIELDING BUNTS

Objective: To teach catchers to field bunts correctly and make a quick, accurate throw to the bases.

Equipment Needed: Full catcher's gear, baseballs, and gloves.

Description: The drill involves catchers working in pairs. One catcher (A) rolls his own bunt to various locations in front of himself, pounces on the ball, and throws to the other catcher (B) who is approximately 60 to 80 feet away. Player A can set up any hypothetical situation he wants. He can throw to first or second base, or position himself in such a way that he can be working for a force-out at third base. After player A throws to B, they exchange roles. Each catcher should make approximately a dozen throws to first base and six throws each to both second base and third base.

Coaching Point:

• The coach should emphasize that the catcher should use his glove in scooping the ball into his throwing hand. The catcher should not attempt to bare hand the ball unless it's the only play he has.

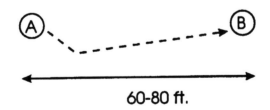

60-80 ft.

DRILL # 61: TAG PLAY AT HOME

Objective: To practice blocking the plate and applying the tag on a sliding runner; to develop the ability to bounce up after a tag play and throw to second base to get a batter attempting to advance to second base on the throw to the plate

Equipment Needed: Full catching gear and baseballs.

Description: The drill initially involves two catchers: one at "home plate" (A) and one approximately 100 feet away (B). The drill begins by having player B throw to the "plate" to A. Player A assumes a position with his left shin guard about a foot in front of home plate in order to block the plate. Player A, however, leaves the outside of the plate "unprotected" for the baserunner to air at with his slide. As he receives the throw, player A quickly gets into a kneeling position with his right knee. Player A holds the ball in his bare hand which he covers with his glove to protect them from the baserunner's spikes. As he catches the ball, player A makes a swipe tag on the imaginary baserunner on the outside of the plate that was offered to the runner. Player A gets the tag "in and out" as fast as possible. Player A then springs up and fires the ball to B who then goes through the same sequence of actions. The drill continues for a preset number of plays.

Coaching Points:

- The drill can be expanded by adding an actual baserunner. In this instance, a coach may want to make the drill more "injury-proof." For example, the drill may be conducted on a grassy area. The baserunner should not wear spikes. The catcher should jeep his mask on to help protect himself during the resulting collision with the baserunner.
- Adhering to the proper mechanics for throwing should be emphasized.
- Variety can be added to the drill by having (B) fungo the ball to (A), instead of throwing it.

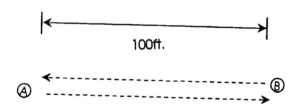

DRILL # 62: STOPWATCH

Objective: To practice making quick, accurate throws to second base. To make catchers more aware of the need to throw quickly.

Equipment Needed: Baseballs, gloves, and a stopwatch.

Description: The drill involves a catcher (A), a pitcher (B), another catcher (C) who serves as the infielder, and a coach. The drill begins by having player B (who is on the mound) throw to A. Player A receives the pitch and throws as quickly and as accurately as possible to C in an attempt to throw out an imaginary baserunner. Player C takes the throw, makes a swipe tag, and tosses the ball back to B. The drill continues for a set number of plays. Using a stopwatch, the coach times player A's throws to second base. From the moment the pitch initially touches player A's glove to when C receives A's throw, the elapsed time should not exceed two seconds.

Coaching Points:

- Throws to first base and third base should also be practiced and timed.
- A "good" time for throwing to second base is under two seconds.

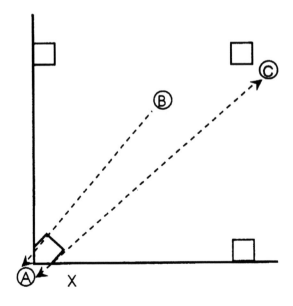

DRILL # 63: PASSED BALL

Objective: To teach catchers to scramble after a passed ball, retrieve it, and make a snap throw from a kneeling position to the pitcher covering home plate.

Equipment Needed: Full catching gear, baseballs, and a home plate.

Description: The drill involves two catchers, both in full gear. One player (A) assumes a catcher's stance in the catcher's box. The other player (B) stands next to home plate. The drill begins by having player A flip the ball behind himself about 20 feet. Player A then races after the ball, slides on his knees alongside the ball, scoops the ball into his throwing hand, and makes a knee-high, snap throw to B who is "covering" home plate. After a preset number of plays, the players switch roles.

Coaching Points:

- Catchers retrieving passed balls should always approach the ball with their glove hand side ready to open up to home plate.
- The key to making a "good" scoop (pick-up) of the ball is for the catcher to get alongside the ball in his slide and to use his glove hand to simultaneously scoop the ball into his (bare) throwing hand.
- Additional players can be involved in the drill by having a third catcher serve as an umpire, a fourth catcher act as a batter, and another player pitch. For example, in this situation, the pitcher (upon a predetermined signal) could throw the ball in the dirt to simulate a passed ball.

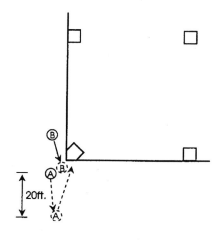

DRILL # 64: POP-UPS

Objective: To practice the techniques and footwork involved in catching pop flies.

Equipment Needed: Full catching gear, baseballs, home plate, and a fungo bat.

Description: The drill involves having a coach hit (or throw simulated) pop-ups around home plate to the catcher. The catcher practices the techniques and fundamentals involved in fielding pop-ups. The catcher's initial step is to remove his mask and locate the ball. He then throws his mask far enough away so that he won't trip over it. On any pop-up, the catcher tries to turn his back toward the infield, because a pop-up off the bat has backspin which will cause it to drift toward the pitcher's mound. The catcher should stay behind the ball and always catch it chest-to-head high, if possible. His hands should be extended about 18 inches from his chest. He should always catch the ball out in front of his body. Using a single-break glove is preferred because it enables the catcher to get his thumb parallel to the ground and underneath the ball.

Coaching Points:

- The drill can be conducted either outdoors or indoors. Outdoors in the sun is preferred. If performed indoors, the drill should involve tossing the ball in the direction of a gymnasium light. The catcher can use either his glove or his bare hand to screen the sun or the gym light while lining up the ball.
- The drill can be expanded to include other players. The coach can hit or throw pop-ups to several players at a time. Players can also hit or throw pop-ups to each other.

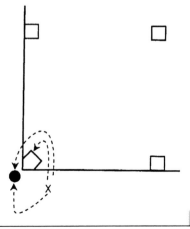

DRILL # 65: FRAMING THE STRIKE ZONE

Objective: To teach catchers to frame and keep borderline pitches in the strike zone.

Equipment Needed: Full catching gear, baseballs, and a home plate.

Description: The drill involves two players: a catcher (A) and his partner (B), preferably another catcher. The drill is initiated by having player A assume his receiver's stance. Standing 25 feet in front of and facing player A, player B points at various locations on the perimeter of the strike zone. Player A extends his glove and catches each "phantom" pitch. The coach watches the action to ensure that player A is working his glove properly and holding pitches in the strike zone. He makes corrections and offers suggestions to player A as needed. Once the basic techniques have been mastered, the drill is expanded to actual throwing. Player A and B throw balls to each other and concentrate on using the proper mechanics and techniques for receiving each throw.

Coaching Points:

- This drill is particularly beneficial in the early weeks of the season.
- The drill should focus on enabling catchers to develop soft hands and the ability to properly frame pitches. Being able to properly frame pitches can make a difference in as much as 25% of the pitches thrown in a game in keeping balls in the strike zone.

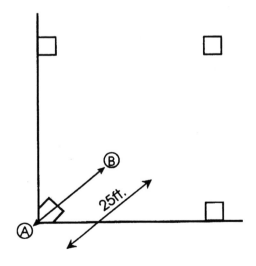

DRILL # 66: FORCE PLAY—DOUBLE PLAY

Objective: To enable catchers to practice making the plate tag on a force-out at home, then stepping quickly toward the pitcher's mound, and throwing to first base.

Equipment Needed: Full catching gear, baseballs, gloves, a home plate, and a first base.

Description: The drill involves three players: two catchers and a first baseman. One catcher (A) serves as the home plate catcher, while the other catcher (B) lines up in the infield, 30 feet in front of A. The first baseman (C) assumes a position on the first base bag, 90 feet from home plate. Player B initiates the drill by throwing the ball to A (who has given him a glove target). Player A places his right foot on the infield edge of home plate and his left foot in front of the plate in a comfortable position. Player A assumes a semi-crouch position awaiting for what he hopes will be a chest-high force-play throw. As soon as he receives the throw, player A pushes off the plate. Using a crow-hop step, he fires the ball to the inside of the first base bag to C. Player A makes 10 plays and then switches positions with B.

Coaching Points:

- If player B's throw to home is wild, A must adjust as needed, tag the plate as best he can, and decide whether he can complete the double play. If he thinks he can't, he shouldn't risk a wild throw.
- If player A is off balance after tagging home, he generally should not throw to first base.

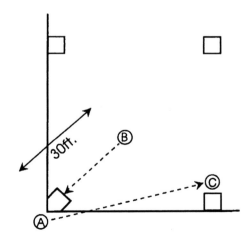

CHAPTER 4

PITCHING DRILLS

DRILL # 67: SAND CAN EXERCISE

Objective: To stretch and strengthen a pitcher's throwing arm. To serve as part of the daily warm-up routine.

Equipment Needed: One sand can per player. (A sand can is a tennis ball can, filled with approximately three pounds of sand, which has been taped at both ends.)

Description: Each player performs each of the exercises illustrated below on a daily basis. Each exercise is done at a relatively slow pace in order to safely force the muscles and ligaments of the throwing arm to perform the desired work/movement. Approximately 10 repetitions of each exercise should be performed.

Coaching Points:

- Sand can exercises should be performed on a daily basis by all team members, not just the pitchers.
- If necessary, the amount of sand in the can may be either increased or decreased as needed. As a result, each player should tape his name on his sand can.

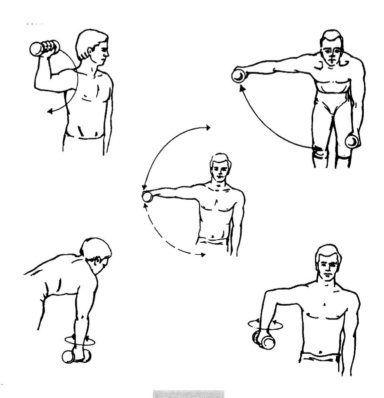

DRILL # 68: SELF-CATCH

Objective: To gain the "feel" of the baseball, and to develop wrist pop.

Equipment Needed: Baseballs and gloves.

Description: Players work individually. Each pitcher "pops" the ball from his throwing hand into his glove hand. The pitcher uses a variety of grips while performing the drill: curve ball, split finger, change ups, cross seam fastball. The wrist snap should be emphasized. The pitchers should attempt to gain a "touch" and "feel" for the baseball. They should experiment with different grips, particularly with the seams.

Coaching Points:

- Many successful coaches and pitchers believe that "wrist explosion or popping" is the most important factor in the mechanics of pitching.
- A pitcher should be encouraged while performing the drill to mentally "pitch a game." He should imagine various situations and react accordingly: for example, two strikes on the batter, baserunners on first and third.
- This drill can be done at home while watching TV or just sitting.

DRILL # 69: CHAIR DRILL

Objective: To emphasize the proper follow-through aspects of pitching mechanics for a pitcher who drags his back legs; to force the pitcher to get his back leg up and over when following through.

Equipment Needed: Baseballs, gloves, and a holding chair.

Description: Only used for those pitchers who struggle getting their back leg up and over when following through, the drill involves two players: a pitcher and a receiver. The pitcher places his throwing (pivot) foot on the seat of a chair (his right foot for a right-handed pitcher; his left foot for a left-handed pitcher), with his toes downward and his heel pointed to the sky. The stride foot should be planted on the ground in front of the chair in a landing position (toe turned in: a closed position). The drill involves having the pitcher practice throwing from this position to his partner who is approximately 30 feet away in a receiver's crouch giving him a glove target. The pitcher throws easy curve balls, while concentrating on pulling his upper body over the thigh of his landing foot.

Coaching Points:

- Particular emphasis in this drill should be put on following through when throwing the curve ball.
- The drill could also involve having the pitcher throw at a target taped onto a net.
- This drill reinforces the baseball expression that throwing a curve requires a pitcher to "pull the body over" or "pull that curve ball down."
- This drill should not involve throwing hard.

DRILL # 70: BAT DRILL

Objective: To practice the proper mechanical sequence of opening the hips and throwing over the stride leg.

Equipment Needed: A bat or broomstick.

Description: The pitcher places the bat behind his back, and holds it in place with his elbows. This action freezes and isolates the pitcher's upper body, enabling him to fully concentrate on properly opening his hips. Starting in a gathered (top of his windup) position, the pitcher then strides toward the plate as if he were pitching. He concentrates on pointing the end of the bat he's holding at the plate for as long as possible before throwing. Then, as the bat turns, his hips have opened. His hips should not open until they reach a point as close to the plate as possible in order to generate maximum power.

Coaching Point:

- When the knee of the pitcher's stride leg begins to rotate toward the plate, his hips will start to open at the same time.

DRILL # 71: BALANCE

Objective: To promote balance; to practice the gathered position; to practice the technique of slightly pausing at the top of the pitcher's windup.

Equipment Needed: Pitcher's mound and baseballs.

Description: The drill involves having the pitcher start his windup without a baseball. When he's in the gathered position, the coach (or another pitcher) places or flips a baseball in the pitcher's throwing hand. As soon as he gets the ball, the pitcher resumes his delivery motion. Initially, the pitcher completes his delivery but does not throw the ball. The drill can subsequently be expanded to have the pitcher actually throw to a receiver.

Coaching Points:

- In order to develop proper balance in his pitcher, the coach can wait any length of time before giving up the baseball.
- During the drill, the coach should stand to the side of the pitcher, toward either first base (for left-handers) or third base (for right-handers).

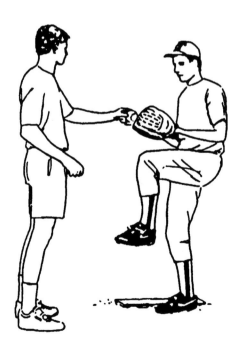

DRILL # 72: PROPER LEG SWING ACTION

Objective: To practice the correct stride-leg action when getting into the gathered (top of the windup) position or from the stretch.

Equipment Needed: None.

Description: The pitcher starts in the stretch position, except that he places his stride foot on the second-base side of his pivot foot. With his stride foot above the rubber, he then lifts his leg somewhat diagonally to the gathered position, pauses, and completes his delivery. By adjusting his foot in this manner, he makes it virtually impossible to swing his leg. The point that must be emphasized in this instance is that the front knee should be brought to the rubber to the gathered (collected) position. In reality, when some pitchers try to get quicker they compromise their level of balance by incorrectly lifting their front leg straight up. In the process, they overlook the fact that proper stride-leg action involves adjusting their weight from the front knee to the back knee.

Coaching Points:

- Some pitchers prefer to swing their stride leg up and back behind them during the pitching motion as opposed to the correct approach of just lifting their stride leg and slightly rotating their hips.
- Leg swinging can cause a pitcher to unduly rush the movement mechanics of his lower body.
- Pitchers who have a serious problem with their stride-leg action mechanics should be encouraged (or required) to perform this on a regular basis until proper stride-leg action becomes a habit.
- This drill also teaches proper stride-leg action when pitching from the stretch in order to prevent the baserunner from a big "jump" when stealing.

DRILL # 73: PROPER FOOT-UNDER-KNEE ACTION

Objective: To practice keeping the foot under the knee during the ball delivery.

Equipment Needed: A folding chair.

Description: The drill involves placing the back of a chair in the path of the pitcher to provide a means of determining whether his lead foot strays too far during his delivery. The pitcher must pitch the ball without kicking the chair. When he is able to throw the ball without his lead foot hitting the chair, his lead foot is in the proper position (very likely under his knee).

Coaching Points:

- Many pitchers prefer to have their foot out away from their body. Such a body position, however, may cause the pitcher to lean backward to compensate.
- Because not keeping his lead foot under his knee during the delivery is a relatively hard habit to break, a pitcher should spend as much time as needed performing this drill.

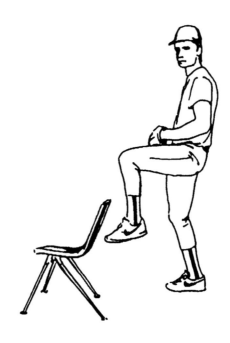

DRILL # 74: PROPER ARM SWING ACTION

Objective: To practice the mechanics of the proper arm swing behind the pitcher's body.

Equipment Needed: Baseballs.

Description: The pitcher kneels on his pivot-leg knee with his stride foot aimed at the plate (target) and his hands together. The drill begins by having the pitcher break his hands. His fingers are on top of the ball. His wrist is cocked toward second base. The elbow of his back arm is elevated above his shoulder. He then watches his arm swing as it goes down, back, and up to the fully extended position. The pitcher should concentrate on keeping his shoulder lined up to the target so no rotation can occur. As a result, his arm is prevented from going behind his body during his pitching motion.

Coaching Points:

- Many pitchers have wasted movement in their deliveries by going back and behind their bodies during the throwing motion. After the break, the pitcher's arm movement should only be down and back (not behind).
- Excessively moving the arm behind his body may result in too much upper body rotation and unwanted arm drag.
- In most instances, the typical reason pitchers swing their arms behind their bodies is they put their hands in the improper position at the top of the windup. The farther away a pitcher's hands are from his body, the more likely he will move his arm behind his body while he is pitching.

DRILL # 75: PROPER FOLLOW-THROUGH ACTION

Objective: To practice full extension and follow-through with the throwing arm; to discourage recoiling the arm after releasing the ball.

Equipment Needed: Baseballs.

Description: The pitcher kneels on his pivot-leg knee with his stride foot aimed at the plate (target). The drill involves having a pitcher simulate throwing a ball (i.e., a dry drill) or throwing the ball at less-than-full speed. After simulating releasing a ball or actually releasing the ball, the pitcher tries to touch the numbers on the back of his jersey in one smooth extension of his arm which moves through the natural route of his follow through.

Coaching Points:

- If a ball is used in the drill, the pitcher can throw the ball either into a net or to a receiver.
- Recoiling the arm after releasing the pitch (which many pitchers, unfortunately, like to do) can lead to a serious injury to the throwing arm.
- This drill should not be performed at full speed under any conditions.

DRILL # 76: "FLAMINGO"—THROWING FROM THE UP POSITION

Objective: To prevent the pitcher from rushing his delivery to home plate. (Note: rushing the delivery is the number one nemesis of all pitchers, and the cause of most sore arms).

Equipment Needed: Baseballs, and gloves.

Description: The pitcher stands sideways to home plate in the stretch position and brings his throwing arm to its highest elevation. He has his glove hand tucked and his landing leg raised and cocked. On command from the coach, he delivers the ball to his pitching partner. The coach calls, "load" or "balance" (pause), "explode" (throw), and "follow through." From this "flamingo" position, a pitcher should be able to throw at approximately 75% of his normal pitching velocity.

Coaching Points:

- When the pitcher rushes his delivery, his body opens up too soon, forcing the path of his throwing arm to take a "shortcut," thereby preventing it from reaching the proper elevation point above his head.
- In taking a shortened course to catch up to his body, the pitcher's arm will pass his head about ear-high, causing him to be wild, up and in.
- When a pitcher rushes his pitches (which many coaches refer to as "throwing only with his arm"), more pressure and strain are placed on his arm because his body "leaves early."

DRILL # 77: JAPANESE CATCH

Objective: To improve a pitcher's control by requiring him to throw strikes from a relatively long distance.

Equipment Needed: Baseballs and gloves.

Description: The pitcher warms up at 75 to 80 feet and reduces the distance gradually until he reaches the normal pitching distance of 60 feet 6 inches. Obviously, the task of hitting the target (the catcher's glove) becomes easier as the pitcher gets closer to the target.

Coaching Points:

- It is recommended that a pitcher make only 20 to 25 throws before he gets to the normal pitching distance.

- Japanese pitchers use this training method to improve their control.

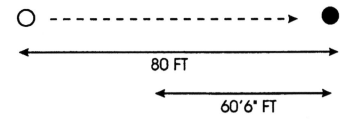

DRILL # 78: CROW-HOP CATCH

Objective: To have the pitcher practice throwing from his back foot in order to help prevent him from rushing his body.

Equipment Needed: Baseballs and gloves.

Description: From 60 to 70 feet apart, two pitchers play glove-target catch, taking a short "crow hop" onto their back foot with every delivery of the baseball. The player receiving the throw should assume a catcher's crouch and give a glove target to the pitcher.

Coaching Points:

- Coaches should emphasize to pitchers to throw from their back foot and not to "rush" their bodies.
- Pitchers should keep their front side closed.
- In most instances, performing this drill for five to 10 minutes is sufficient.

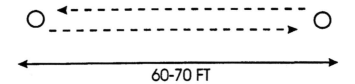

60-70 FT

DRILL # 79: WALL BALL-RUBBER BALL GAME

Objective: To practice pitching and work on control.

Equipment Needed: A rubber ball of regulation size and weight, chalk, a home plate, and a wall.

Description: A strike zone is drawn on a concrete wall in chalk. On each side of the strike zone, an outline of an imaginary batter is also drawn. The drill involves having a pitcher set up at the proper pitching distance (60′ 6″) from the wall. He then pitches an imaginary game against the wall, using all of his pitches and his imagination. He keeps the count, outs, innings, and score.

Coaching Points:

- The pitcher can throw as many innings as he chooses.
- The drill figuratively allows a pitcher to throw in a "competitive" game any day he wishes . . . and be a winner.
- The drill can be expanded to allow two pitchers to oppose each other. They can alternate innings and keep score. For example, they can go five innings or 60 to 70 pitches each, whichever comes first.

DRILL # 80: GAME CONDITIONS

Objective: To improve the pitcher's concentration and selected mental aspects of pitching by simulating game conditions.

Equipment Needed: Gloves and baseballs.

Description: The drill involves three players. After properly warming up, the pitcher pitches a simulated game against a stand-in batter. The third player acts as the catcher. Every aspect of the simulated game is regulation, with the batter alternating as left- or right-handed hitters. The stand-in hitter protects himself by using his glove. If the ball is thrown too far inside, the batter catches it and gives it to the catcher. Prior to each pitch, the catcher gives the sign and location to the pitcher and sets up in his catching stance. The pitcher pitches his (simulated) game until he has thrown a prescribed number of innings or pitches as predetermined by his coach.

Coaching Points:

- Several baseballs should be available to conduct the drill, so that if a pitch gets past the catcher, the drill can be continued while the ball is being retrieved.
- Sufficient rest should be allotted between successive repetitions of the "game conditions" drills.

DRILL # 81: INTRA-SQUAD PRESSURE PITCHING

Objective: To provide pitchers with the opportunity to learn how to handle pressure situations they may have to face during the season.

Equipment Needed: Baseballs, gloves, bats, and bases.

Description: The team should be divided into two groups: one on offense and one defense. The drill involves creating as many situations as possible with the offense trying to score and the defense trying to shut them out (late innings, ball-strike counts, runners on base, and ninth-inning jams). The pitcher has to pitch appropriately for each situation. The primary focus of the drill is to provide a competitive environment which allows pitchers to be better prepared for the season.

Coaching Points:

- The pitchers should not be overworked. As a general guideline, each pitcher should be limited to throw three to four innings maximum.
- The main emphasis of the drill is to create the "end game."
- Begin each hitter with a 1-and-1 count to create the need for more strikes to be thrown by the pitcher, and the need for the hitter to swing at the first good pitch.

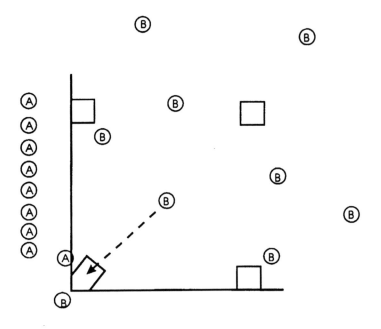

DRILL # 82: QUICK AS A CAT

Objective: To practice the basic mechanics of pitching quickly from the stretch position with a runner on first in a stealing situation; to teach the pitcher to throw quickly to either first or home.

Equipment Needed: Stopwatch, balls, and gloves.

Description: The basic focus of this drill is to develop maximum quickness in both a pitcher's delivery to home and his throws to first base. The general procedures for conducting the drill are relatively simple. Using a "glide step," the pitcher (A) delivers (throws) the baseball to home as quickly as he can, or fires the ball to the first baseman (B) as quickly as he can. His coach times the throws and calls out the times to him.

Coaching Points:

- A "good" time from the mound to the catcher is 1.3 seconds from the time the pitcher breaks his hands until the ball touches the catcher's mitt.
- A "good" time from the pitcher to first base is 1.1 seconds or better. A snap throw from a right-handed pitcher to first base is often as low as .9 or .8 seconds.
- The key for a right-handed pitcher is quick feet and short-arm movement. The key for a left-handed pitcher is quickness and deception.

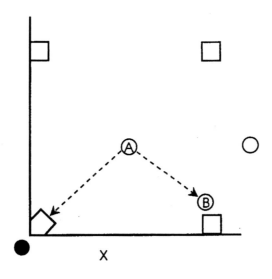

DRILL # 83: PEPPER-DOUBLE PLAY

Objective: To practice starting the 1-6-3 double play; to develop quick feet in the turn to second base; to practice making an accurate, chest-high throw to the middle infielders on the 1-6-3 double play.

Equipment Needed: A bat, baseballs, and gloves.

Description: The drill involves three players, all of which can be pitchers. One player (A) is the pitcher. A second player (B) serves as a hitter. The third player (C) acts as a middle infielder. The drill begins with player A pitching to B who is standing approximately 30 feet in front of him. Using a choke grip, player B attempts to hit a ground ball up the middle right back to A. Player A fields the ground ball, wheels, and throws to C who is standing at "second base" (approximately 60 feet behind A.) Player C then returns the ball to A, and the drill is continued. After 10 plays, the players rotate positions. The drill continues until each player has had 20 opportunities to make the play.

Coaching Points:

- The players should constantly be reminded to "speed up the drill."
- The emphasis should be on having a pitcher cleanly field the ground ball and then turn and make a strong, chest-high throw to second base.

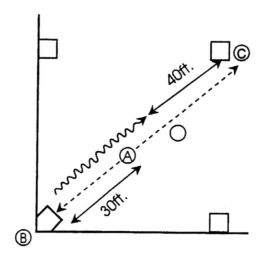

DRILL # 84: INFIELD SITUATION FUNGOS

Objective: To practice the skills and techniques required to respond to various infield "game" situations.

Equipment Needed: Baseballs, bats, and gloves.

Description: The drill involves using a complete infield to work on various infield situations. An extra pitcher serves as the batter. The coach calls out the play he wants (for example, bunt situations, squeeze play situations, or double play situations). The pitcher delivers a pitch and the batter fungos the play. The key to the drill is to keep the ball in the infield and to create every possible situation at some point during the drill. In most instances, the drill should be performed for approximately half an hour.

Coaching Points:

- If enough pitchers are available, they can run to first base after the ball is fungoed, creating an even more game like situation.
- Variety can be incorporated into the drill by using outfielders as hitters and, subsequently, as baserunners.

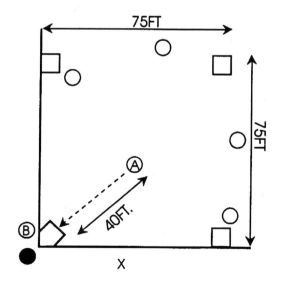

DRILL # 85: WALL PEPPER

Objective: To improve a pitcher's fielding techniques and skills; to enable a pitcher to develop "good hands."

Equipment Needed: Rubber balls of regulation size and weight and a wall.

Description: The drill involves one or more pitchers, each working alone. Each pitcher stands approximately 25 to 30 feet from the wall and throws a rubber ball against the wall so that the ball rebounds off the wall to create all sorts of ground balls. In his mind, the pitcher should envision a variety of baseball "game" situations. Depending on the simulated situation, he can then wheel back for the imaginary double play, field bunts, or throw to imaginary bases.

Coaching Points:

- The drill could also be conducted using two or more players simultaneously. One player could throw the ball off the wall and call out the "play," while one of the other players would then field the ball off the wall.
- Traditionally, this drill is a very popular, particularly among kids in urban areas who have spent considerable time playing baseball in the streets.

DRILL # 86: "V" PICK-UPS

Objective: To improve lateral quickness, develop stamina, practice fielding, and work on the footwork involved in wheeling and throwing to a base.

Equipment Needed: Baseballs, gloves, and two cones.

Description: The drill involves two pitchers: one who serves in the field (A) and one who acts as a hitter (B). The two players stand 15 feet apart. A reasonable width is marked off with cones for player A to cover—approximately 10 feet to his right and 10 feet to his left. The drill begins by having player B firmly roll a baseball to A's right or left without letting A know which direction he's going to roll the ball. As the ball is rolled, player B calls out a base—first, second, third, or home. Player A then scoops up the ball, wheels and feigns a throw in the direction of the base which B called out. The thrower may also drop a bunt straight ahead and have player A charge, field the ball, and throw it where directed. The fielding pitcher should return to the middle of the two cones after every chance. After a preset number of chances, the two players exchange roles.

Coaching Points:

- The drill should be kept moving.
- The drill can be varied by adjusting either the distance between the players or between the cones.

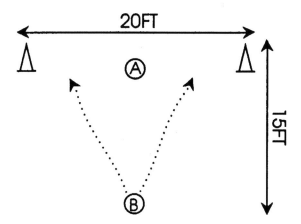

DRILL # 87: TWO-MAN PICK-OFFS

Objective: To practice accuracy, quickness, and footwork in pick-off throws to each base.

Equipment Needed: Baseballs and gloves.

Description: The drill involves having two pitchers work together on their pick-off throws at a distance of 45 to 50 feet. Each player concentrates on developing the proper footwork and making quick, accurate throws.

Coaching Points:

- This drill should be performed every day by the pitching staff.
- This drill can also be conducted without a ball in order to save the pitchers' arm, especially if they have pitched recently.

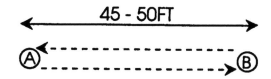

DRILL # 88: TEAM PICK-OFFS

Objective: To practice making strong, accurate throws; to involve the infielder on pick-off plays, and to work on solid team defense.

Equipment Needed: Baseballs and gloves.

Description: The drill involves a complete set of infielders, and each at his position, and four pitchers (A) positioned adjacent to the mound working at the same time delivering pick-off throws to each base. Each infielder works on his pick-off signs, moving to the bag to receive the throw, tagging, and returning the ball to the pitcher who threw him the ball. Home plate is treated as another first base station. The catcher acts as a first baseman. After six throws to each base, the players rotate. Depending on the number of pitchers available, at least two rounds of the drill should be performed.

Coaching Points:

- Good defensive teams practice pick-offs at each base until eventually they master the necessary techniques.
- Variation # 1: Outfielders can be incorporated into the drill as lead-off runners; they should not attempt to return to the base on pick-off throws because of the potential of being hit with the throw.
- Variation # 2: The drill can also be conducted without baseballs. This procedure can help save the pitchers' arm and allow baserunners to practice getting back to a base, or break for the next base, without the danger of being hit by the ball.

DRILL # 89: RIGHT SIDE PLAYS

Objective: To improve the ability of infielders to make plays on balls hit to the right side that require the pitcher to cover first.

Equipment Needed: Fungo bat, baseballs, and gloves.

Description: The drill involves a coach, 4-6 pitchers (A) alternating on the mound, and both right side infielders (the second baseman (B) and the first baseman (C)). The drill begins by having the coach hit fungo ground balls to the right side of the infield. The ball is fielded by either the first baseman or the second baseman. After the ball has been hit, the pitcher hustles to a specific aiming point where he catches the ball and tags the bag. The pitcher's aiming point is six to eight feet in front of the first base bag, slightly up the line. The pitcher stays inside the baseline, looking for the ball before he reaches the bag. He then tags the inside of the bag, while keeping his head down to make sure of the tag. After tagging the bag, he pivots back toward the center of the diamond to see if another runner is trying to advance a base.

Coaching Points:

- This drill requires both work and timing.
- The coach should occasionally lay down a drag bunt between the first baseman and the mound. Both the pitcher and the first baseman should go for the ball. If the pitcher fields the bunt, he should try to beat the runner to first base since he is aware of the fact that because the first baseman also went for the ball, he will not be in a position to cover the bag. On the other hand, if the first baseman fields the ball (because the ball went past the pitcher), he should then shovel the ball to the pitcher. The pitcher already has momentum toward the bag and is often in a reasonable position to beat the runner to first base.

DRILL # 90: GLIDE STEP

Objective: To enable pitchers to develop quickness in throwing the ball either to home plate with a runner in stealing position or to first base.

Equipment Needed: Baseballs and gloves.

Description: The drill involves three pitchers. The pitchers form a triangle, approximately 45 feet apart. The drill begins by having the pitcher with the ball wheel and make a pick-off throw to home (to the player on his left in the triangle) or use a glide step and throw to home (to the player on his right in the triangle). The player who receives the throw then goes into his stretch and repeats the sequence of the drill (throwing either to first or home). Conducted on a continuous basis, the drill should be timed by the coach.

Coaching Points:

- The pitcher should be made aware of the importance of being able to throw quickly to both first base and home. He should be able to throw to first in one second or less. Although left-handed pitchers usually rely more on deceptiveness, they should be able to make a snap throw to first base in approximately one second.
- From the time the pitcher breaks his hands from the stretch position to the time the ball hits the catcher's glove, no more than 1.3 seconds should elapse. Such a goal can only be accomplished if the pitcher uses a good glide step.

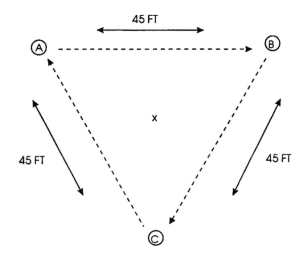

DRILL # 91: CALLING FOR THE POP-UP

Objective: To enable pitchers to practice handling short pop flies in the infield, and allowing the appropriate infielder to field a high pop fly which has been hit over the pitcher's mound.

Equipment Needed: Baseballs, gloves, and fungo bat.

Description: The drill involves a complete set of infielders, including the catcher, who are in position. The coach hits fungo pop-ups in the infield area, both fair and foul. Priorities are established, enabling decisions to be made on who will catch the ball.

Coaching Points:

- Pitchers must learn to make good judgments on pop flies and get out of the way.
- On short pop-ups, the pitcher may be in the best position to catch the ball. Accordingly, he should call out and make the play.
- If the catcher loses the ball in the lights or the sun, the pitcher should be ready to make the catch.
- Some coaches may allow a pitcher to catch all of the pop-ups hit to his area if he is the best athlete.

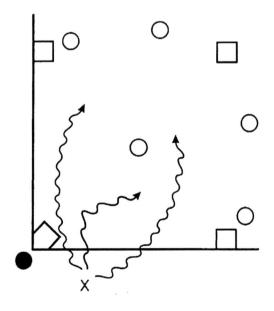

DRILL # 92: PASSED BALL

Objective: To practice receiving a throw from the catcher and applying a tag on the runner who is sliding into home plate from third, without having the ball kicked out of the pitcher's glove; to enable catchers to practice making throws on short passed balls to pitchers who are covering home plate.

Equipment Needed: Baseballs and gloves.

Description: The drill involves two players: a pitcher and a catcher. Standing approximately 30 feet in front of the catcher, the pitcher throws the ball in the dirt to his catcher. The catcher allows the ball to get past him. The catcher then races after the ball, slides to it, quickly picks it up, and from his knees, throws it to the pitcher who is covering the plate. The pitcher straddles the plate, leaving a portion of the plate "uncovered" for the runner to slide into. Upon catching the ball, pitcher slaps a tag onto an imaginary runner. He then gets his glove hand up and out of the way of the runner as quickly as possible.

Coaching Points:

- The pitcher should be careful not to block the plate without the ball. A runner might bowl him over, an action that could result in a serious injury to the pitcher.
- The drill can be expanded by incorporating a baserunner. In this instance, the drill should be conducted on grass with the baserunner running at half-speed. Full-force collisions should be avoided at all costs.

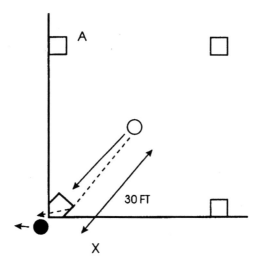

DRILL # 93: GLOVE POINT GAME

Objective: To improve a pitcher's control.

Equipment Needed: Baseballs, gloves, and moveable rubber home plates.

Description: The drill involves groups of three players: two pitchers and a catcher. The pitchers pair off, taking turns throwing to the catcher from the mound. The catcher gives five specific targets: high and low inside; both outside corners; and the center of the strike zone. The pitchers deliver the ball to the catcher's glove. Once he is able to repeatedly hit his target, the pitcher changes the type of pitch he is throwing (fastball, curve, or change-up) and continues throwing. The pitchers throw equal numbers of pitches from the windup and stretch positions.

Coaching Points:

- The drill can be varied to increase player interest by setting up a point system. Each pitcher receives one point per strike. The first player to earn 15 points wins. The catcher judges whether a pitch is a strike or not.
- The drill can also be made more difficult by eliminating the center of the strike zone, making it a "no-no" zone. As a result, only pitches on the corners count as strikes.
- Catchers should be reminded to give a clear target, holding their mitts steady. A moving target can create confusion and many cause the pitcher to lose his concentration.
- The drill can be performed either indoors or outdoors.

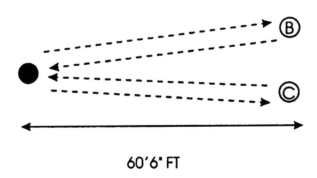

60'6" FT

CHAPTER 5

PICK-OFF PLAY DRILL

DRILL # 94: PICK-OFF BASIC RUNDOWN

Objective: To teach the first baseman to make a quick accurate throw to second base after the pitcher has picked-off the baserunner at first base, and the base- runner has broken for second base; to have infielders practice the rundown play.

Equipment Needed: Gloves, bases, and baseballs.

Description: The drill involves four players: a pitcher (A), a first baseman (B), a middle infielder (C), and a baserunner at first base (D). The drill begins by having the pitcher make a throw to the first baseman to pick-off the baserunner. The first baseman then fires the ball to the middle infielder in an attempt to get the baserunner who was picked-off. He then follows his throw in case there is an ensuing rundown. He and the middle infielder execute the rundown play. The baserunner attempts to avoid the tag and get either back to first or down to second. After a reset number of plays, the players switch positions.

Coaching Points:

- The coach should emphasize to the first baseman that the baserunner should be tagged out as quickly as possible.
- The coach can incorporate competition into the drill by having the two fielders run sprints or perform push-ups every time the baserunner is able to get back to the base safely.

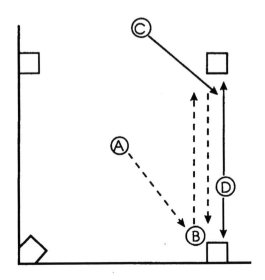

CHAPTER 6

BUNT DEFENSE DRILLS

DRILL # 95: DRAG BUNT DEFENSE

Objective: To teach the first baseman and the pitcher the techniques involved in fielding a drag bunt.

Equipment Needed: A base, gloves, and baseballs.

Description: The drill involves three players: a pitcher (A), a first baseman (B), and another player who serves as a feeder. The pitcher and the first baseman line up in their "normal" positions. The feeder sets up adjacent to home plate. The drill begins by having the feeder roll the ball in the area between the pitcher and the first baseman, simulating a drag bunt. The pitcher and the first baseman make an instant judgment that the pitcher may not be able to handle the bunt. As a result, the pitcher realizes that the first baseman must race in and attempt to field the ball. At the same time, the pitcher continues trying to field the bunt. If he does field the ball, he scoops it up and races to beat the baserunner (the feeder) to the bag. If the pitcher can't reach the ball, the first baseman must field it and shovel it to him. In the latter instance, the pitcher takes the toss from the first baseman, continues on to first base, and tags the bag.

Coaching Point:

- In either instance, the pitcher should make the play at first because his momentum is already in that direction. On the other hand, because the first baseman is charging in toward the plate to make the play, he would have to brake himself and change directions.

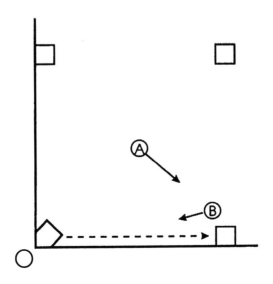

DRILL # 96: BUNT DEFENSE—FIRST BASEMAN

Objective: To have first basemen field bunts and practice throwing out runners at all the bases, including home.

Equipment Needed: A base, baseballs, and gloves.

Description: The drill involves two first basemen and a position fielder. One first baseman (A) acts as a batter. The drill begins by having player A standing approximately 90 feet away (at home plate) roll a bunt toward the other first baseman (B). Player B breaks in and fields the ball, wheels and throws to the fielder (C), who is positioned at a pre-designated base. Player B should make five throws to each base, including home plate (to simulate making the squeeze play), and then exchange places with A.

Coaching Points:

- The drill can be expanded by adding one or more baserunners.
- The player acting as the batter (A) should vary the location and the speed of the simulated bunts he rolls to the first baseman (B).

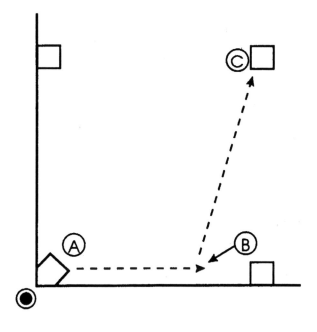

DRILL # 97: BUNT DEFENSE—BASERUNNER AT FIRST BASE

Objective: To have infielders practice defending against a bunt when a baserunner is on first base; to practice baserunning and sliding techniques.

Equipment Needed: A bat, baseballs, and gloves.

Description: The drill involves having a full set of infielders, including the pitcher, at their regular defensive positions. The rest of the team divides into two groups. One group acts as hitters (A), while the other group serves as baserunners (B). The first player in the hitter's line is at bat and the first man in the baserunner's line is on first base. The drill requires that the fielders must defend against four possible bunt situation scenarios. Each scenario begins by having the pitcher throw to the hitter who must bunt the ball (anywhere he chooses) and then attempt to beat out the bunt. In the first scenario, the defense fields the bunt and throws the ball to first base which is covered by the second baseman. The second baseman checks the baserunner who has advanced to second base to see if he has rounded the base too far. In the second scenario, the defense fields the bunt and again throws the ball to first base to the second baseman. In this situation, the second baseman quickly fires the ball to second base in an attempt to get the baserunner, who has rounded the base too far. In the third scenario, the defense fields the bunt, but this time throws the ball to second base to the shortstop who is covering the base in an attempt to turn the double play. In the fourth scenario, the defense fields the bunt and throws the ball to first base to the second baseman. The second baseman then fires the ball to third base in an attempt to get the baserunner, who is attempting to advance to third base from first base on the play.

Coaching Points:

- The coach and his assistants should critique each player's performance to ensure his adherence to proper techniques.
- If the pitchers can't throw strikes or the batter can't bunt fairly, the coach can roll out a simulated bunt.

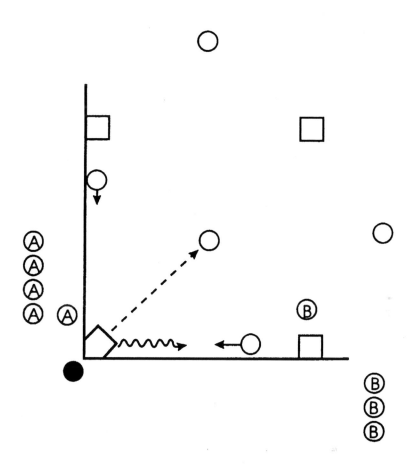

CHAPTER 7

DOUBLE STEAL DEFENSE DRILLS

DRILL # 98: DOUBLE STEAL DEFENSE—
BASERUNNERS AT FIRST AND THIRD, THROW TO HOME

Objective: To have the catcher practice throwing accurately to second base with a runner on third; to practice faking the runner at third base and throwing accurately to the infielder who has coverage; and then practice throwing to the base runner from first base who is attempting to steal second base.

Equipment Needed: Full catching gear, bases, baseballs, and gloves.

Description: The drill involves four players: two baserunners (one at first base (A) and one on third base (B), a catcher, and a middle infielder (C)). The drill begins by having the catcher feign receiving a pitch and announcing, "GO." At that point, the baserunner who was on first base starts for second base which is covered by the second baseman or the shortstop. The catcher then throws the ball to the second baseman. Simultaneously, the baserunner on third breaks for home. The second baseman then throws the ball back to the catcher in an attempt to get the runner coming home from third base. If the third baseman sees the baserunner on third break for home, he yells, "Home." On the other hand, if the middle infielder feels that the baserunner at third base has wandered too far from the bag, he can throw directly to third in an attempt to catch the baserunner off the bag before he can safely get back.

Coaching Points:

- Whoever has the best arm between the second baseman and the shortstop (usually the shortstop) has bag coverage on plays at second. The only time the shortstop does not have bag coverage at second is when a dead-pull, right-handed batter is at the plate.
- In this type of double-steal situation, we employ a communication system where the catcher's signal dictates the action that will be taken. If the catcher calls "1," he throws to the pitcher; if he calls "2," he throws to second base; if he calls "3," he throws to third base; and on a "4" call, he executes a full-arm fake.
- The drill can be performed without a ball (phantom style) in order to minimize any strain on the catcher's arm. Each player involved in the drill just goes through the motions—no ball is actually thrown.

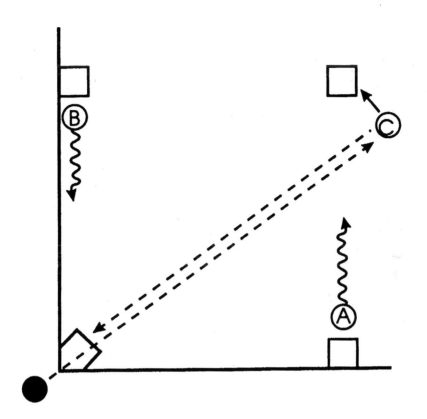

DRILL # 99: DOUBLE STEAL DEFENSE:
BASERUNNERS AT FIRST AND THIRD—CUTOFF THROW TO HOME

Objective: To practice the cutoff throw-to-home special play for defending against the possible first and third double steal.

Equipment Needed: Full catching gear, bases, baseballs, and gloves.

Description: The drill involves five players: two baserunners (one at first base (A) and one at third base (B), a catcher, and two middle infielders (a shortstop (C) and a second baseman (D)). With the double steal a possibility, the catcher signals to the middle infielders that he wants to put on a special double steal defensive play. If a right-handed hitter is in the batter's box, the catcher will fire the ball out to the second baseman, who will race in from his normal position to the lip of the infield grass to catch the throw from the catcher. Even though a baserunner is breaking for second, the second baseman does not go toward second base at all. The catcher then fires the ball directly to the second baseman. Hopefully, the baserunner at third base will see the ball go past the pitcher's mound and fail to notice the change in the defensive alignment for receiving the throw. If the baserunner on third base then breaks for home, he should be an easy out on the return throw from the second baseman to the catcher. If a left-handed hitter is at the plate, some coaches believe that the same procedures should take place, except that the catcher's throw should now be directed to the shortstop who has also assumed a drawn-in position on the lip of the infield grass. All factors considered, a better option might be to throw the ball back to the pitcher (instead of the shortstop) when a left-handed hitter is at the plate.

Coaching Points:

- The drill can be performed without a ball (phantom style) in order to minimize any strain on the catcher's arm. Each player involved in the drill just goes through the motions—no ball is actually thrown.
- The defense must become the aggressor in baserunners-on-first-and-third, double-steam situations.
- First-and-third, double-steal situations demand a lot of practice time to master properly.

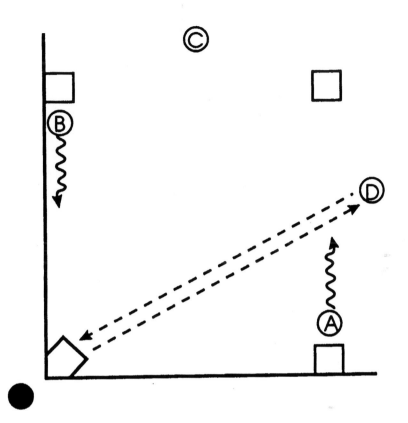

DRILL # 100: DOUBLE STEAL DEFENSE:
BASERUNNERS AT FIRST AND THIRD, READ AND THROW

Objective: To practice reading the situation with baserunners at first base and on third base in a double steal situation and making an appropriate throw.

Equipment Needed: Full catching gear, bases, baseballs, and gloves.

Description: The drill involves six players: two baserunners (one at first base (A) and one at third base (B)), a catcher, a third baseman (C), a middle infielder (D), and a pitcher (E). The drill begins by having the pitcher from a shortened distance (approximately 30 to 40 feet away) throw a pitch to the catcher. If the third baseman feels that the baserunner on third has gone too far down the line, he throws both of his hands in the air and moves to a position approximately three feet inside the baseline, parallel with the third base bag. Anytime the catcher sees the third baseman's hands raised, he then throws to the inside of the base (trying not to hit the baserunner in the back) to the third baseman who attempts to make the tag play on the baserunner who is scrambling back to the bag. The catcher can throw directly to third without first faking a throw to second base, or he can fake a throw to second base, take a short crow hop, and then fire the ball to third base. In actuality, the play is dictated by the catcher (refer to the communication signaling system discussed in Drill # 98). In this scenario, play #3 (i.e., the catcher throws the ball to third base) is particularly effective when a left-handed hitter is at the plate.

Coaching Points:

- The drill can be performed without a ball (phantom style) in order to minimize any strain on the catcher's arm. Each player involved in the drill just goes through the motions—no ball is actually thrown.
- The defense must become the aggressor in baserunners-on-first-and-third, double-steal situations.
- First and third, double steal situations demand a lot of practice time to master properly.

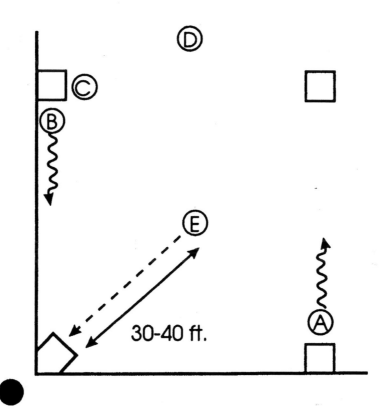

30-40 ft.

DRILL # 101: DOUBLE STEAL DEFENSE—
BASERUNNERS AT FIRST AND THIRD

Objective: To have the catcher practice looking at a baserunner who is on third base, trying to freeze him, and then throwing out the baserunner from first base who is attempting to steal second base.

Equipment Needed: Full catching gear, bases, baseballs, and gloves.

Description: The drill involves four players: two baserunners (one on first base (C) and one on third base (D)), and two catchers—one positioned behind the plate as a receiver (A) and one serving as a middle infielder (B) to cover second base. The drill begins by having player A feign receiving a pitch. With a ball in his hand, player A then looks at third, freezes the runner, and fires the ball to B at second base to throw out the baserunner from first base who is attempting to steal second. After a preset number of plays, he players rotate positions.

Coaching Points:

- The drill can be performed without a ball (phantom style) in order to save stress on player A's arm. Everyone just goes through the proper motions— no ball is actually thrown.

- The drill can also involve giving the catcher various options: for example, on the first play he can freeze the runner at third and then hold the ball; on the second play he can freeze the runner at third and then throw the ball to second base; on the third option, he can freeze the runner at third and then actually throw to third; and finally, he can full-arm fake to third and hold onto the ball.

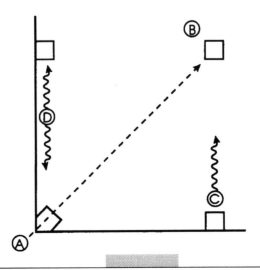

Pat McMahon is the head baseball coach at the University of Florida. One of the most respected coaches in the game, success has followed McMahon at every destination. He assumed his present position at Florida in 2001 after serving four years as the head baseball coach at Mississippi State where he led the Bulldogs to a College World Series appearance in 1998, two consecutive NCAA Super Regional Berths (2000 and 2001), four straight NCAA Regionals and a 164-88 overall record. In 2001, his squad won the SEC Tournament title, finished 39-24 and advanced to NCAA Super Regional play for the second straight season. In nine years as a head coach at both Mississippi State (1998-2001) and Old Dominion (1990-94), he amassed a 353-174 record and .670 winning percentage. In just a relatively short period of time, McMahon already ranks among active college baseball coaching leaders in winning percentage.

McMahon took over the Mississippi State baseball program in 1998 after three seasons as an associate head coach under MSU head coach Ron Polk. It was the first of four successful years McMahon would spend in Starkville. In his first season, McMahon was named the AVCA South Region Coach of the year after guiding the Bulldogs to the College World Series in 1998. He became just the second coach in SEC history to lead a school to the CWS in his initial season in the league. The 1999 season saw the Bulldogs win 13 straight games, finish 42-21 overall and advance to NCAA Regional play. In 2000, the McMahon-led Bulldogs finished 41-20 overall, hosted and NCAA Regional and advanced to NCAA Super Regional play before losing to Clemson. In 2001, he guided a youthful squad with four freshman All Americans to a 39-21 record, the school's first SEC tournament title since 1990, and MSU's second consecutive NCAA Super Regional Berth. He concluded his four-year MSU head coaching tenure with a 164-88 record and led the SEC with 37 SEC Academic Honor Roll recipients. In addition, 20 of his players were selected in the Major League Baseball draft.

A graduate of Stetson University, McMahon began his collegiate coaching career as a graduate assistant coach in 1980 at Mississippi State. He then moved on to Old Dominion as an assistant coach for two seasons and helped lead the Monarchs to their first-ever NCAA Tournament berth in 1982 before returning to Starkville as head coach Ron Polk's chief assistant/ pitching coach from 1983-89.

From 1990 to 1994, McMahon guided Old dominion to newfound prominence and unprecedented levels of success including two NCAA regional appearances, two school-record 40+ win seasons and an outstanding 189-86 record. His 1994 squad sported a 40-14 overall record, won the Colonial Athletic Association regular season title and advanced to the NCAA Regionals. That year he was honored as coach of the year in both the CAA and the state of Virginia. McMahon then moved back to Starkville and Mississippi State as Polk's associate head coach in 1995.

McMahon and his wife, Cheri, have two children — a daughter, Logan, and a son J. Wells.

James A. Peterson, Ph.D., FACSM, is a sports medicine consultant and freelance writer who resides in Monterey, California with his wife, Sue. He is the author of over 70 books and 200 published articles on a variety of subjects. Among the books he has helped write are *Competitive Leadership* with Brian Billick and *Finding The Winning Edge* with Bill Walsh and Brian Billick. He has long been active as a fellow of the American College of Sports Medicine and as a voluntary fundraiser for the Make-a-Wish Foundation.